PATRIOTIC
GRACE

ALSO BY PEGGY NOONAN

John Paul the Great:
Remembering a Spiritual Father

A Heart, A Cross, and a Flag: America Today

When Character Was King:
A Story of Ronald Reagan

The Case Against Hillary Clinton

Simply Speaking: How to Communicate Your
Ideas with Style, Substance, and Clarity

Life, Liberty, and the Pursuit of Happiness

What I Saw at the Revolution:
A Political Life in the Reagan Era

PATRIOTIC GRACE

What It Is and Why We Need It Now

PEGGY NOONAN

Author of *A Heart, A Cross, and a Flag*

Collins

An Imprint of HarperCollinsPublishers

PATRIOTIC GRACE. Copyright © 2008 by Peggy Noonan.
All rights reserved. Printed in the United States of America.
No part of this book may be used or reproduced in any
manner whatsoever without written permission except in
the case of brief quotations embodied in critical articles
and reviews. For information, address HarperCollins
Publishers, 10 East 53rd Street, New York, NY 10022.

HarperCollins books may be purchased for educational,
business, or sales promotional use. For information, please
write: Special Markets Department, HarperCollins
Publishers, 10 East 53rd Street, New York, NY 10022.

FIRST EDITION

Library of Congress Cataloging-in-Publication Data is
available upon request.

ISBN: 978-0-06-173582-0

08 09 10 11 12 DIX/RRD 10 9 8 7 6 5 4 3 2 1

To United States Senators John McCain
and Barack Obama; to former United States
Senators Slade Gorton and David Boren;
and to Tim Russert, who bridged many gaps.

"What do we mean by patriotism in the context of our times? . . . A patriotism that puts country ahead of self; a patriotism which is not short, frenzied outbursts of emotion, but the tranquil and steady dedication of a lifetime. There are words that are easy to utter, but this is a mighty assignment. For it is often easier to fight for principles than to live up to them."

Adlai Stevenson, New York City
August 27, 1952

"I've always believed that a lot of the trouble in the world would disappear if we were talking to each other instead of about each other."

Ronald Reagan
April 11, 1984

ACKNOWLEDGMENTS

These were in my Higgins boat:

Adam Bellow, Suzanne Gluck, Julie Cave, Tonya Newman, Sarah Ceglarski, Terry Teachout, Michael Novak, Frank Petito, Stephanie and Ransom Wilson, Eric Lupfer, Michael Santorelli, ladies group, Romans Group, James Taranto, Brendan Miniter, Paul Gigot, Sim and Lisa Johnston, Charles Perry Wilson, Anne and Bruce Williams, Gary Press, Steve Ross, Bruce Nichols, Nancy Miller, Ruth Mannes, Kate Antony, and Will Rahn. Blended into this book are pieces of columns that have appeared in the *Wall Street Journal*.

PATRIOTIC
GRACE

PROLOGUE

The View from Gate 14

Where is America?

America is on line at the airport. America has its shoes off, is carrying a rubberized bin, is going through a magnetometer. America is worried there is fungus on the floor after a million stockinged feet have walked on it. But America knows not to ask. America is guilty until proven innocent, and no one wants to draw undue attention.

America left its ticket and passport in the jacket in the bin in the X-ray machine, and is admonished. America is embarrassed to have put one one-ounce moisturizer too many in the see-through bag. America is irritated that the TSA agent removed its mascara, opened it, put it to her nose, and smelled it. *Why don't you put it up your nose and see if it explodes?* America thinks, but does not say.

And, as always America thinks: Why do we do this when you know I am not a terrorist, and you know I know you know I am not a terrorist? Why this costly and embarrassing kabuki when we both know the facts, and would even admit privately that all this harassment is only the government's way of showing that it is "fair," of demonstrating that it will equally humiliate anyone in order to show its high-mindedness and sense of justice? Our politicians congratulate themselves on this as we stand in line.

All the frisking, beeping, and patting down is demoralizing to our society. It breeds resentment, encourages a sense that the normal are not in control, that politics has lessened everything, including human dignity. Another thing: it reduces the status of that ancestral arbiter and leader of society, the middle-aged woman. In the new fairness, she is treated like everyone else, without respect, like the loud ruffian and the vulgar girl on the cell phone. The middle-aged woman is the one spread-eagled over there in the delicate silk blouse beneath the removed jacket, praying that nothing on her body goes beep and makes people look.

America makes it through security, gets to the gate, waits. The TV monitor is on. It is Wolf Blitzer. He is telling us with a voice of urgency about the latest polls. But no one looks up. We are a nation of Willy Lomans, dragging our wheelies through acres of airport, walking through life with a suitcase and a slack jaw, trying to get home after a long day of meetings, of moving product.

No one in crowded Gate 14 looks up to see what happened with the poll. No one. Wolf talks to the air.

Gate 14 is small-town America, a mix, a group of people of all classes and races and ages, brought together and living in close proximity until the plane is called. Our town appears, the plane is boarded, the town disappears. An hour passes, a new town begins. This is the way of modern life. We live in magic and are curiously unillusioned.

Gate 14 doesn't think any of the candidates is going to make their lives better. But Gate 14 will vote anyway, because they know they are the grown-ups of America and must play the role and do the job.

But here's something they notice, we notice. Our leaders are now removed from all this, removed from life as we live it each day.

There is as I write broad resentment toward President Bush, and here is one reason: a fine and bitter sense that he has never had to stand in his stockinged feet at the airport holding the bin, being harassed. He has never had to live in the world he helped make, the one where Grandma's hip replacement is setting off the beeper over here and the child is crying over there. And of course as a former president, with the entourage and the private jets, he never will.

Nor will Bill Clinton, nor the senators and leaders who fly by private jet.

I bet a lot of Americans, most Americans, don't like it. I'm certain Gate 14 doesn't.

✫

All this is part of the mood of the moment. It is marked in part by a sense that our great institutions are faltering, that they've forgotten the mission; that the old America in which we were raised is receding, and something new and quite unknown taking its place; that our leaders have gone astray. There is even a feeling, a faint sense sometimes that we have been relegated to the role of walk-on in someone else's drama, that as citizens we are crucial and yet somehow . . . extraneous.

But we are Americans, and mean to make it better. We long to put the past few years behind us, move on, and write something good on the page we sense turning.

This little book, written on the eve of a great election, without knowing how it will end, is intended to remind us of who we are, where we have been, where we are now, and where we are headed—together.

PART ONE

This happened to my friend John, an average American kid from New Jersey who grew up in Montclair in the 1930s and '40s. I stress average. He kept a pigeon coop in the backyard, weeded lawns for ten cents a bucket, and went to the local public school.

When World War II began, John joined the navy, and in May 1944, at the age of twenty-two, he was an ensign on the USS *Thomas Jefferson*, a former luxury liner that had been converted to an assault vessel. There he was placed in charge of five of the landing craft for the invasion of Europe.

Each would carry twenty-five soldiers from the *TJ*, as they called it, onto the shore of France. John's landing site was to be a fifty-yard stretch of shoreline dubbed Dog Red Beach. It fell near the middle of Omaha Beach, which was pretty much the center of the assault.

The *TJ* sailed to England's Portsmouth Harbor, which was jam-packed with ships. On June 1, the army troops arrived, coming up the gangway one by one. "They were very quiet," John said when he told me his story in July 2008. Word came on June 4: the invasion would begin that night. They geared up, set off, but were ordered back in a storm. The next morning, June 5, the rain was still coming down, but the seas were calmer. So about 8:00 that night they cast off to cross the channel. The skies were dark, rain lashed the deck, and the *TJ* rolled in the sea. At midnight they dropped anchor nine miles off the coast of France. The men were summoned to a big breakfast, eggs and ham. At 2:00 a.m. the crew began lowering the landing craft, called Higgins boats. The Higgins boats were thirty-six feet long, rectangular, flat bottomed, "a kind of floating boxcar, with head-high walls." A crane would lower them over the side, and the soldiers would climb down big nets to get aboard. "They had practiced, but as Eisenhower always said, 'In wartime, plans are only good until the moment you try to execute them.'"

The Higgins boats pitched in the choppy water. The soldiers, loaded down "like mountaineers," with rifles, flamethrowers, radio equipment, artillery parts, tarps, food, and water, "seventy pounds in all," had trouble getting from the nets to the boats. "I saw a poor soul slip from the net into the water. He sank like a stone. He just disappeared in the depths of the sea. There was nothing we could do."

So they improvised, deciding to board the Higgins boats on the deck of the ship, and hoist them, full, into the sea. John scrambled into a boat with his men, and the crane lifted it, but the boat got caught on the *TJ*'s railing and almost tipped over and tumbled the men into the water. They held on for dear life. Just at that second a wave came and righted the ship, which untangled the boat, and they were lowered safe into the sea.

It took John's five little boats four hours to cover the nine miles to the beach. "They were the worst hours of our lives. It was pitch black, cold, and the rain was coming down in sheets, drenching us. The boats were being tossed in the waves, making all of us violently sick. We'd all been given the big breakfast. Hardly anyone could hold it down. Packed in like that, with the boat's high walls. A cry went up: 'For Christ's sake, do it in your helmet!'

"Around four a.m. the dawn broke and a pale light spread across the sea, and now we could see that we were in the middle of an armada—every kind of boat, destroyers, probably the greatest array of sea power ever gathered."

Now they heard the sound, the deep boom of the shells from the battleships farther out at sea, shelling the beach to clear a path. And above, barely visible through clouds, they saw the transport planes pushing through to drop paratroopers from the 82nd and 101st Airborne divisions. "Those were brave men."

At 5:00 a.m. they were close enough to shore to recognize some landmarks—a spit of land, a slight rise of a bluff. In front of them they saw some faster, sleeker British boats trying desperately to stay afloat in the choppy water. As the Americans watched, three of the boats flipped over and sank, drowning all the men. A British navigator went by in a different kind of boat. "He was standing up, and he called out to my friend in a jaunty British accent, 'I say, fellows, which way to Pointe du Hoc?' That was one of the landmarks. It was expected to be the toughest beach of all. My friend yelled out that it was up to our right. 'Very good!' the man cried out, and then went on by with a little wave of his hand." John later doubted the man had lived another hour.

Closer to shore, a furious din—"It was like a Fourth of July celebration multiplied by a thousand." By 6:00 a.m. they were eight hundred yards from shore. All five boats of the squadron had stayed together, a triumph in those conditions. The light had brightened enough that John could see his wristwatch. "At six twenty, I waved them in with a hard chop of my arm: Go!"

They faced a series of barriers, heavy metal rods. They made a sharp left, ran parallel to the shore, looking for an opening, got one, turned again toward the beach. They hit it, in a foot or two of water. The impact jarred loose the landing ramps to release the soldiers as planned. But on John's boat, it didn't work. He scrambled to the bow, got a hammer, and pounded the stuck bolt. The ramp crashed down and the soldiers lunged forth. Some were hit with shrapnel as they struggled through to the beach. Others made it to land only to be hit as they crossed it. The stuck ramp probably saved John's life. After he'd rushed forward he turned and saw, to his horror, that the man who'd been next to him the whole trip, the coxswain to whom he'd barked orders—"Hard to port, make it smart, we'll look for an opening!"—had been hit by an incoming shell and decapitated. The shell likely would have hit John too if the bolt hadn't stuck and the door hadn't jammed and he hadn't run for the hammer.

The troops at Omaha Beach took terrible fire. Half the soldiers from John's five boats were killed or wounded. "It was a horrible sight. But I had to concentrate on doing my job." To make room for the next wave of landings, John raised the ramp, backed out, turned around, and sped back to the *TJ*. "I remember waving hello to the soldiers in the incoming boats, as if we were all on launches for a pleasure cruise. I remember thinking how odd that such gestures of civility would persist amid such horror."

Back at the *TJ*, he was told to take a second breakfast in the wardroom—white tablecloths, steward's mates. It was surreal, "from Dog Red

Beach to the Ritz." As he ate he heard in the background the quiet boom of the liberation of Europe. Then back to a Higgins boat for another run at the beach. This time the ramp lowered, and he allowed himself to get off.

Dog Red Beach was secure, littered with wrecked landing craft of every kind. The bodies of the dead and wounded had been carried up onto a rise below a bluff. He felt thankful he had survived. "Then I took a few breaths and felt elated, proud to have played a part in maybe the biggest battle in history."

John went on to landings in Marseilles, Iwo Jima, and Okinawa. After he came home he went to work at a relatively small Wall Street investment firm called Goldman Sachs, and in the next fifty years he went on to chair it, to work in Ronald Reagan's State Department, and to head great organizations such as the International Rescue Committee. He is, in that beautiful old phrase, a public citizen.

But if you asked him today his greatest moment, he'd say that day on the beach, when he was alive and young and had done something dazzling. "At that moment, dead tired, soaked to the skin, I would not have wanted to be anywhere else in the world."

When I asked John Whitehead why he had done what he'd done, he spoke of things you've heard before—patriotism, a young man's excitement at wearing the uniform, an acceptance of the idea of sacrifice. And something else.

One day, as a teenager, just before or just after the war began, he saw something amazing. He was swimming off the Jersey Shore with his friends, and suddenly there, peering up from the waves, was the periscope of a submarine. A German submarine, surveying the American shore. The sight amazed and shook him. America was under threat. It needed his protection.

It was a straight line from that moment to Red Dog Beach.

Why do we tell these stories? Because tales of courage move us, inspire us. Because we long for greatness, and wish to know the specific facts and data of a heroic act so we can fix it more firmly in our minds. Because our country is more divided now than it was then, and it comforts us to think of a time when we were united, and did something great.

And maybe we tell these stories because it helps us to remember that John and the hundred thousand other Americans of D-Day were pretty much regular guys, average people we could know, or be.

And this is important because on some level we know history isn't done with us yet, history never is, and we will face great challenges, too. We wonder if we're up to it, if we'll be equal to the moment if the moment is big.

Some of our doubts in this area are realistic. Some not.

For instance: We look back at the Greatest Generation and its tales of war, woe, and triumph, and we sigh a great sigh. "They're not making 'em like that anymore." They were great, we are not, end of story. But is that true? We're still making humans, yes? Still pretty much with the same ingredients? Man's composition hasn't changed. And we are still Americans. We are what old Pope John Paul called us when he first visited America: a good people, and brave.

And maybe we're more united than we think. We're on our way to work each day, to the office, the store, the hospital, rattling forward in our own little Higgins boats, the car, the train, the bus, and we think we're alone but . . . we're not. Others are taking that beach too, trying not to be hit, trying to forge ahead. Now and then the clouds lift and you see: We are an armada. All sorts of Americans, wonderful people, all ages, faiths and colors, with different skills, fabulous skills, from a million different places, but all here with you, going forward. We love our country, love our kids, want to lead good lives. And what burdens we carry. Talk about being loaded down like mountaineers! There is suffering and heart-break in every family you know, and so much grace, and endurance. Sudden sickness, accidents. The sheer daily weight of meeting the mortgage, keeping the job. *"For Christ's sake, do it in your helmet!"* Baby, we do that every day.

We are more heroic than we see.

And we let odd little things get in the way of seeing it. For instance, the idea of generationism, that one group of us born at a particular time is better than another born at a different time.

Chances are pretty good the man or woman leading your own little group of Higgins boats is not
one of the Greatest Generation, not one of those
who suffered and fought but—brace yourself for
the insult, for the sheer demoralizing fact of it—
a Boomer, born after the war, during the baby
boom.

That huge demographic force, seventy-six
million strong, the famous basketball in the py-
thon, born, according to the population experts,
between 1946 and 1964, aged now forty-four
through sixty-two. They are running America
still, in positions of authority in the media, the
academy, politics, medicine, the sciences, foundations. The youngest of them will be running
America for another generation, as those born in
the '70s and '80s come up.

And this is obviously bad for all of us, for the
Boomers are very dreadful. Shallow, selfish, soft,
the worse of the "istics": materialistic, narcissistic,
pessimistic.

You know what I'm talking about, you've seen
the stylish essay in the plodding newsweekly,
we've all seen it the past ten or twenty years:
"Boomers: Bad." One should note that these

pieces have tended to be written by Boomers themselves, but by a particular sort, a quadrant of the generation: those who had relatively easy lives and don't seem to like how they've turned out. They came from homes that were affluent, stable, suburban; their parents guided them to Yale right quick. They were lucky, and good for them, and maybe the arc they always describe applied to them: they were idealistic, according to their lights, and then careerist, enjoying power and money, and then one day at Williams Sonoma they bought a brushed-steel home-brew espresso maker imported from Italy, had a flashback to their joyous, innocent rolling in the mud at Woodstock, and realized they were . . . bad. And maybe when they wrote their essays they were not so much reporting as projecting; maybe they don't hate their generation, maybe they just hate themselves. And maybe they're right! Who are we to second-guess?

But they shouldn't have roped the rest of us into their self-condemnation. And members of the Greatest Generation, in a moment of sustained mischief, should not have echoed the charge and reinforced it. It was ungracious of them. You know who first called them the Greatest Generation, and made movies about them, lauding them in essays and speeches? The Boomers, in a moment of generational grace.

So, it is absurd to say that one generation is "great" and the one that follows is not, silly to say that someone born in 1920 is, by virtue of that fact, better than someone born in 1960. And Boomers have allowed all this to leave them with less pride than they are due.

I know Boomers and I am one, and let me tell you, they are not weak, not cynical, and they are tough enough. The ones not in the magic quadrant worked their way through school as waitresses, secretaries, salesgirls on the floor of the shop on Main Street, and removers of thorns from roses in the flower shop. (I held these jobs and learned from all but the last, which just left my hands nicked and raw.) They went to college at night, worked as deliverymen and office temps and attendants. They became the fire captains who ran into the burning towers, they were the generals of the Surge, they became Mom and Dad keeping the family together. A Boomer e-mail, circa July

2008: "Everything is okay—Holly and Scott are very happy, no money, he's in a full MBS program, no job. She's in dissertation phase and makes a little tutoring. Candy and Jay are in love but no plans as yet. Mom is in a nursing home, temporarily. She's on oxygen 24/7 now due to emphysema. I'm looking for lawyers right now to help Dad settle things—they need to move out of the house or get someone in full time. I am extremely stressed. Oh stop already this is like a soap opera." The writer of that e-mail, quoted exactly except for a change in names, is my best friend from sixth grade, who, with her husband, supports everyone in their family financially, and they are the only "generation" in the family that never whines, that does and expects to do the grunt work, that gives money up and down, and that works like a rented mule to do it. You know why she complained to me? Because she doesn't complain to anyone else. She's a Boomer.

They didn't have World War II? They had Vietnam, where two million of them fought, where fifty-eight thousand of them died, and the ones who went there, most of them, went knowing no one would thank them, there would be no parades when they returned. No estimable member of the Greatest Generation was going to write for them, "These are the boys of Co Ka Leuye. These are the boys who took the ridge."

They had 9/11 and its recovery. They led people out of the towers. They forged up the stairs, weighted down like mountaineers, with seventy pounds of gear. They lined up outside St. Vincent's hospital waiting for wounded to save, stoic when they understood, at the end of the day, that there would be no one to treat, that they were all in the smoke. They lifted the New York Stock Exchange covered with ash—the monitors on the floor literally thick with ash, the trading floor badly damaged—and one week later, seven days, they were lined up ready to roar and ringing the bell. That day, for the first and only time in my life, I bought a stock—five thousand dollars worth of J&J—and as I bought it on the Internet, I called my son over to watch me hit Enter so he would understand for the rest of his life that when America is in trouble you invest in it, you put what you've got right there. We became stockholders in America, Inc. There's a commercial now that shows a new American family, Asians, having a similar moment with the computer and then hitting Enter. A Boomer probably wrote it. We are a sentimental lot.

The great prosperity that has swept our country the past quarter century? The Boomers were the grunts of the great abundance, the junior officers now in command. Want to see our routing sheet? We dropped anchor at Dow Jones 1,000 in '75, and made it to Dow Jones 12,000 today. We. Created. Jobs. You're welcome.

We paid for the government programs the Greatest Generation passed on for us to pay for. Then we created our own and passed them on, too. And not all of us had so much. Some of us had little and gave our children much. We were idealistic, and not only in the "Flower Power" way, the "Make Love, Not War" way. A lot of us were actually working too hard to get to the demonstration. We were idealistic in the Peace Corps way, the raise-a-family way, the become-involved way. We still are. You have a local church? Who runs it, heads the clothing drive and the food bank? That would be a Boomer, right?

We came to early adulthood in a crime wave, teenagers when it began and early middle-agers when it ended. You know why it ended? We were the cops.

You might say we were the last generation to grow up with statues—statues in the church, statues on the green. St. Joseph with a carpenter's tool in his hand over there near the row of red candles; General Patton there on the field at West Point. We found them stirring. By saying we were the last to grow up with statues, I mean we were the last—so far!—to feel awe at them, awe for the things they represented. We understood the concept of greatness. We were children in 1958 and 1965 and we felt moved by history and its makers. And we had to hold on to that, because the art all around us as we came into maturity was, suddenly, all rusted I-beams, rocks, and twisted steel. The person had been removed from art. All was abstraction, and human nobility— human presence!—had been banished. After the building of the Vietnam War Memorial in Washington, Boomers pressed, hard, for the creation of the stirring Frederick Hart statue of the Three Soldiers struggling forward. It's beautiful, a complement to and concretization of the meaning of the Wall. Perhaps now the Boomers of Long Island and Queens will rise up against the abstractionists and theory people who are creating the memorial at the World Trade Center, with their spare and arid symbolic evocations of . . . something or other. Perhaps some hardy Boomers will insist on the inclusion of the one thing everyone in their hearts knows belongs there: a statue of a company of doomed firemen looking upward, toward the burning towers in which they knew, as they said at the funerals, they were about to take the "stairway to heaven."

Children now seem not so stirred, not by the statues in the church and not by the statue of Patton. "He's the one who slapped the soldier, isn't he?" "Isn't that . . . George C. Scott?" Their awe is contained.

Ours was not. The Boomers were the last to feel the old stirrings, at least for now, at least so it appears. And good, because we'll need it. We'll have to bring it into the future with us.

I mount this little defense because we can be rather tough, rather unappreciative of each other in our Higgins boats. We can be tough on the young, too. They come into the office on the internship, the junior fellowship, they're low on the totem pole, and let's face it, we look right through them, tagging them as ill-educated refugees from expensive schools, forgetting to teach them the ropes, forgetting, sometimes, that *we're* their teachers, *we're* the ones introducing them to professional life, *we* have to make up for some of what the world forgot to teach them, and give them examples of how to live. We should be saying, through our actions, *Come in, come in, we do good things here.* They have been shaken by the world since 9/11, and we don't understand how rocked they've been. They've internalized it; they never talk about it. But: They are not always sure they have a future. They can't imagine the coming decades as rosy, seamless, full of expansion. They are something new in America, an entire generation that does *not* assume their lives will be even better than their parents.' Pollsters think this is all about money, global competition, economic instability. I don't think that's what it's about.

You notice I haven't referred to this generation by a name. Others have come up with them and nothing's quite stuck, and good. Let them not have a label. Let's call them Americans. They're in the Higgins boat too, as we barrel toward unknown shores.

What are we barreling toward?

A difficult time, I think.

I came to see this in a new way on the hot, sultry afternoon of June 9, 2004. I was in Washington, D.C., for the funeral of Ronald Reagan. About a hundred of us, his old cabinet chiefs, party elders, and those who'd worked with him, had come together in the Mansfield Room, a grand ceremonial room on the Senate side of the U.S. Capitol. My son was with me. He would turn seventeen in two days. I wanted to expose him to history. I had no idea how much history he'd see.

An Air Force 747, one of the two used as Air Force One, had been sent to California, to the naval air station at Point Mugu, following Reagan's death; it was about to bring his flag-draped coffin to Andrews Air Force Base, in Maryland. There, a cortege would take him to the Capitol, where we, and the senators and congressmen now massing in the Rotunda, would receive him. Afterward he would lie in state, and a mourning public would come in numbers so great—more than a hundred thousand, many of whom had camped out overnight on the sidewalks—that it would startle sophisticated observers who knew how much time had gone by, and how people forget.

So there we were, in the Mansfield Room. There was some laughter—it wasn't sad; our friend had lived a long and fruitful life, and had been liberated from long illness—and remembering. "Remember the time in Geneva . . ." "Were you in Washington when Jack Kennedy lay in state?" Over here George Shultz, Reagan's secretary of state. Jack and Joanne Kemp, members of the 1970s economic movement that spurred the '80s economic revolution. Richard Allen, Reagan's first national security adviser, and Judge William Clark, his second. Ed and Ursula Meese, from the early days, in California. Paul and Carol Laxalt, part of the Western conservative rebellion that spread like a prairie fire in the '70s. In a corner, Senator Pete Domenici watched the TV monitors by himself, with tears in his eyes. Near him, tall and gray, Hugh Sidey of *Time*, historian of presidents.

It was like seeing a portion of the Old America, of people who'd been raised in the '30s and '40s and '50s and who knew, had been formed by, that vanished place. The gold-trimmed walls, paneled in black walnut, bore portraits of George Washington—a Gilbert Stuart, the Pennington portrait—and of Mike Mansfield, pipe in hand. I stood aside and watched, looking at one point toward the big entranceway that led to an arched, high-ceilinged hall. Near it, a handsome young man in a white jacket was handing my son a ginger ale. My son had just taken the drink when a rude man rushed by and knocked the glass from his hand.

Only he wasn't a rude man. He was a frightened man, and he was trying to save our lives.

He walked quickly and heavily and placed himself a few feet into the room. He had on a brown wool sports jacket.

"Excuse me! Excuse me!" he barked.

The old lions looked at him, and turned away. They must have thought him an excited functionary sent to tell us the body would soon land at Andrews. They continued talking.

"Quiet! Quiet!" He was ordering them now. I

was standing just to his left, and when he said "Quiet" the first time, I saw something. His voice was under control and his face was inexpressive, but his carotid artery, just above his collar, was pounding. I could see it throbbing.

As this thought registered—*something is wrong*—he said, "We are evacuating the Capitol! Now! This is not an exercise! We are evacuating. Leave the Capitol. Now."

People looked startled, began to leave, and my eyes met my son's. I walked toward the doorway and took his arm. Already in the halls there was running and loud talk, scores of people rushing by. Someone in a uniform called out, "Incoming unidentified aircraft, sixty seconds out!"

We were moving quickly now, down the hall, toward an exit that led to the great steps of the Capitol.

There, at the top of the steps, someone yelled, "Aircraft incoming!"

As we hurried down the Capitol steps a guard yelled, "Run for your lives! Ladies, take off your shoes, run for your lives! Go north. North!"

At the bottom of the steps, still holding my son's arm, I turned. There, at the top, in front of the huge, shadowed entranceway, was Oatsie Charles, in her wheelchair. Eighty-four years old, a fabled Washington social figure, pillar of the old Georgetown, friend to presidents from JFK on. I know her only slightly, and yet she symbolizes for me the old bipartisan Washington, an old social ideal. She was stranded, unable to move forward, as people rushed past. Her grandnephew Nick was by her side, but he couldn't get her down alone. And just as I saw this, two burly uniformed officers came, stood at each side of her wheel-chair, and hoisted it up. They carried her down the long steps as she sat, looking straight ahead, her cane in her right hand, held aloft like the brave little prow of a ship.

My son and I waited for Oatsie, and Nick, a graduate student at Georgetown, and when they reached the bottom we moved on together. Two more friends joined us. By now perhaps ninety seconds had passed from the time we'd been told to evacuate. A Capitol Hill cop was yelling, "This way, this way!" We paused, strategized. What we needed was a big solid place, away from here. Union Station, a few blocks away, go. So we ran and pushed, and inside the station we saw a bar and scrambled in, and in the bar we found out Washington was not under attack.

It was all a mistake. A plane had strayed over Capitol airspace; it had ignored warnings never received. It was carrying a Southern governor going to the funeral. He didn't even know he'd almost been shot down.

We settled in around a wooden table and Oatsie, asked by a waiter for her order, coolly waved her hand: Your very best chardonnay, dry, if you can. And then she told my son of the first president she had ever seen, Franklin D. Roosevelt, who went by in a big black convertible one day when she was young. She spoke of Jack and Jackie and the high, impossible snows of that bracing inaugural day. And we watched, together, the arrival of Ronald Reagan at Andrews Air Force Base on a Sony Jumbotron in the corner of the bar.

But something had happened as I watched Oatsie being carried down the Capitol steps. A thought had come with the force of an intuition, though it was not that, just a thought, barely carried in words. In time it sank in, and did not leave me for months, and then years.

It was:

Before this is over we'll all be helping each other down the stairs.

Just that.

Before this is over . . .

It came to be for me a reordering thought. I'd felt a version of this sentiment since 9/11, and maybe you did too. But in some new way, for me, it . . . broke through. And stayed with me, coming to reshape or reorient my thinking, my attitude, about many things.

I came to think this: the old ways are over, the old politics are over. The weary going through the motions as each side brutalizes the other: over. A new time has begun, or must begin. We have to sober up, we have to change, the stakes are that high. This is a time for seriousness, for high-mindedness, forbearance, and reason. We have to try to sort of shake our heads and see each other new, and the landscape new.

The "this" in the sentence—"before this is

over . . ."—refers not of course to the moment I'd witnessed at the Reagan funeral but to the larger age we live in, the era we occupy. The "all" is all of us Americans: geniuses, muddleheads, old people and young, liberals and Democrats, conservatives and Republicans, and the radical and the bland, and people who've never heard of politics. Little babies. Wicked men at the top of their game. All.

We know we live in an age of weapons of broad and immediate destruction, that they can be harnessed and deployed against civilian populations by any group with the will, money, and mad focus to do it. An age of many enemies, and freelance actors, as they say, and gifted grievance groups. Of individuals and associations capable of making, or getting their hands on the makings of, these weapons. It is an age of portable nukes, biochemical weapons, biological entities, an age of nation-states that can send missiles containing warheads across oceans. We talk about this, and we argue about it in a specific sense—it's al Qaeda or another terror group; it's Korea, or Iran, or China. I believe the immediate challenge comes, and will come, from the fascistic excitements and tropism toward violence of sects within funda-mentalist Islam. But the point of this small book isn't who, but what.

I believe we have to assume that something bad is going to happen, someday, to us. Maybe it will be ten years from now, but maybe not, maybe sooner, much sooner. We have to assume, I think, that it will be a 9/11 times ten, or a hundred, or more, and that it will have a deeply destabi-lizing effect on our country; that it will test our unity and our endurance, our resourcefulness and faith.

We all know this, I think, deep down. I don't know a major political figure in America to whom all this has not occurred, and often. We've read the books, seen the movies, heard the warnings. Google "Washington as terror target" and you get 9 million hits; "New York and terror target" gets 9.5 million. I know, I just did.

And yet in some deep way our politics do not reflect our knowledge. It's odd. Stunning, actually.

We keep going through the same old motions in the bitter old ways. Even our cynics are not being realistic!

"Man has never developed a weapon he didn't ultimately use," Ronald Reagan once said in conversation in the Oval Office. He spoke, in his soft voice, of the great horror of modern warfare, that civilians are now targets. Once they weren't. Now they are.

It worried him. It worries me.

And that is only the external threat. The domestic ones are all around us, in the air, and we know them well: Will the banks fail, is the system built on anything but faith, and will the faith hold? Will we keep our coherence as a country, will we hold together, can we continue as a sovereign nation at peace with itself?

These are big questions, and in a funny way too I think they're in the back of our minds, but we don't regularly allow them into the front because . . . well, it's all too big, and I've got a mortgage to pay, and while I keep my part of the democratic bargain—I work, pay my taxes, and take care of my family—I've got to assume the government is doing its part, which is taking care of all the big questions I can't answer.

But I think we also wonder: *Is* anyone really in charge? Is there a grown-up in the house? This,

I believe, is the true legacy of Hurricane Katrina: Our leaders, our mayors and governors and presidents, are pretty good at talking on TV and saying inspirational words, and at being charming in the Green Room, their real psychic home. And yet when the floodwaters rise and people take to the roofs and the looting begins they're . . . no more competent than you or me. Less, actually. That was the demoralizing thing: less. Even though this is what we hire them for, the baseline responsibility we give them: to maintain the public safety, to defend the nation.

I said the thought I had after seeing Oatsie carried down the stairs was a reordering one. It was so because in some new way I came to see a future hard time as not just an inevitability but a *central fact*, the one that, when we look back on this era, will give it its central shape and meaning. The fact by which history will judge our current actions.

In the beginning, this left me feeling a deeper tenderness toward all of us—*Poor lost people, poor incompetent us! Dancing in the stateroom as the iceberg looms!* But in time it left me feeling in a deeper way, so deep it became reflexive, that the Americans all around me, whoever they are, whatever their philosophy, whatever their views, are my future comrades. They'll be helping me down the stairs; I'll be helping them. Why not, to the extent it is possible, cut to the chase? Why not help each other in the ways we can, to the extent we can, now?

I am a political conservative, but liberals are my future comrades, and if you are a liberal, conservatives are yours. They'll be helping you down the stairs. We're going to get through the difficult times as Democrats and Republicans together, as Americans together. We knew this in our bones after 9/11. But time passed, things happened, and we forgot.

I came to think our pointless enmity must end. On both sides, all sides. In some new way we had to get out of the political and into a new sphere, the patriotic. The partisan gamesmanship, the focus-group cynicism, the base-playing: There's only one base now, and it is our country.

All this came to change the way I do my work, which is writing about politics. It left me—it is a little embarrassing to say this, because it admits and acknowledges a previous lack—open in some new way to, and eager to hear, the stands and suggestions of those I'd previously seen as generally unhelpful (that would be liberals), and sometimes newly protesting of some of the actions of those whose views I'd previously found congenial. I tried to express some of this in a piece I wrote in 2006, when I began a new column, called "Declarations," in *The Wall Street Journal*. "Autumn is the true American New Year," I wrote. "This is when we make our real resolutions. The perfect fall has two things, present pleasure (new exhibits, shows, parties) and something to look forward to—for the political, the upcoming election. Which is my subject. My resolution is to try in a renewed way, each day, and within my abilities, to be fair. I find myself thinking so much of William Meredith's poem about the advice he'd received from older writers: 'Look hard at the world, they said—/ generously, if you can / manage that, but hard.'"

This naturally won me a bop on the head from a Democratic blogger, who held it as evidence of previous bad faith. But you have to start somewhere.

✻

In all this I am not saying, to paraphrase Rodney King, Why can't we all just get along? We can't because we're human: something's wrong with us. But we can do better.

I don't mean "we must outlaw politics," or "splitting the difference is always best." Politics is a great fight and must be a fight; that is its purpose. We are a great democratic republic, and we struggle with great questions. One group believes *A* must be law, the other *Z*. Each side must battle it through, and the answer will not always be in the middle. The answer is not always *M*.

But we can approach things in a new way, see in a new way, speak in a new way. We can fight honorably and in good faith, while—and this is the hard one—both summoning and assuming good faith on the other side.

To me it is not quite a matter of "rising above partisanship," though that can be a very good thing. It's more a matter of remembering our responsibilities and reaffirming what it is to be an American.

If nothing else, this means we must now have

our fights over *big* issues, issues of real consequence that are pertinent to the moment we're in. We shouldn't be fighting and hitting each other over the head over little things, stupid things, needlessly chafing ones. When I would think of this the past few years I'd always return to one thing, a prime example of the old way of doing politics. This was the movement, now quiescent, to alter the Constitution of the United States to outlaw . . . flag burning. Imagine changing that great document for such a stupid thing. As if it meant anything if an idiot burned a flag; as if a lot of idiots were even burning flags—which they weren't, and aren't. I called it a movement, but of course it wasn't: it was a political game played by one team in order to embarrass the other. *"He doesn't love our flag—he won't even protect it!"* Boo! goes the crowd.

And yet the oddest thing is . . . the crowd knows it's being played. They know their buttons are being pushed. And this doesn't leave them feeling more inspired by, more trusting in, the system. So much of our silliness is, in the end, destructive.

• • •

And so I came to think this: What we need most right now, at this moment, is a kind of patriotic grace—a grace that takes the long view, apprehends the moment we're in, comes up with ways of dealing with it, and eschews the politically cheap and manipulative. That admits affection and respect. That encourages them. That acknowledges that the small things that divide us are not worthy of the moment; that agrees that the things that can be done to ease the stresses we feel as a nation should be encouraged, while those that encourage our cohesion as a nation should be supported.

I've come to think that this really is our Normandy Beach, or rather our Red Dog Beach, the little, key area in which we have to prevail if the whole enterprise is to succeed.

The challenge we must rise to.

So where are we now? I yank this into the present to look at the landscape on which a rise to the challenge is possible, but not, I'm afraid, very likely.

It is autumn, and America is picking a president. It has been exciting. The whole year was confounding, putting the professional political class in its place, leaving the experts scratching their heads, and giving us all the feeling—so precious, so rare—that the people are in charge. They make the decisions, not pollsters. And you never knew what they'd do next. John McCain was over and done a year ago, out of money and out of luck. And then: he wins the nomination. Barack Obama was unknown and outmatched a year ago, sure to be a victim of someone else's inevitability. Well. *Nothing is inevitable.* And he wins the nomination.

A year of marvels. And now two men, McCain and Obama, each worthy in his way of admiration, battle it out. Neither seems by nature inclined toward brute, gut-player politics. One, McCain, had been hurt by it in the past, his presidential prospects in part done in by it in the Republican primaries of 2000. He has a temper, and at some point he'll have shown it, but the ugly road, I think, embarrasses his pride. The other, Obama, seems temperamentally not inclined to be a killer, to encourage the dark side of politics.

It's not his history: he took down a machine without raising his voice.

So neither man, I think, will prove in this respect to be . . . embarrassing. In March of 2008, I was on Jon Stewart's show as yet another person talking about the election year, and during the commercial, Stewart expressed relief at the bottom-line respectability of the likely nominees. Yes, I said, it's like the coming year won't be . . . disgusting. It was the only word I could think of, and it startled us and made us laugh.

However.

Something tells me that the election will already be showing itself to be rough indeed, if not because of the candidates themselves then very much because of their surrogates or would-be surrogates—a million freelancers and operatives, YouTube Fellinis, and political action committees.

Two huge teams are in a massive public brawl in an era in which the Internet has liberated everyone in the country from the old restrictions, the old establishment, the old, encrusted media monopoly. Good. A short, smart piece by an un-

known writer on an obscure blog can, if the links
are lucky, be seen by more eyes than the report of
the mainstream media journalist at a major newsweekly who only ten years ago was just getting
used to being asked for his autograph in restau-
rants.

It's all led to a new parity. It has allowed serious new voices to emerge. In fact, at the moment,
that is one of the headlines on the Internet, that
the blogosphere hasn't so much degenerated into
an intellectual Wild West as it has encouraged
new and independent thinking and testimony.

As for YouTube, it has yielded, this year, the
most moving and wittiest advertisements about
each of the candidates. Professional political con-
sultants with their piece of the buy didn't produce
them, artists did. For Obama, it was the video by
will.i.am, with the Obama speech and the snatches
of song made from his words. More than anything else this year, it captured the feeling behind
his movement. The McCain video, alas, was anti-
McCain, and keyed off the will.i.am video. It fea-
tured young people and artists taking snatches of
McCain speeches, turning them into song, and
then starting to . . . freak out as they listened to

the words. It made you laugh out loud. Anyway, one of the untold stories of the year is the failure of the political professionals to compete with the art and brightness of the nonprofessionals.

But nothing good comes without price, and the Internet has also unleashed, or rather given a stage to, the polar, and the destructive. They speak anonymously on comment threads, in e-mails, and because they don't have to put their names to what they say, they don't have to stand by their views. In this sense they are cowardly and should feel shame. But they're also powerful in that they successfully unleash certain toxins into the political air. They feel pride. They've changed things. There probably isn't a major institution in Washington right now that doesn't have staffers jumping into the fray, slamming the foe, starting e-mail chains, comment threads, and mass-blasting their opponents.

This is a great new fact of American politics, and it has grown exponentially since 9/11. It has come not only to have an impact on public debate but, in some ways, to drive the way our politics is done. And we both know this and don't know it.

It crept up on us; we've acclimated ourselves to it; but we're still getting used to what it is doing to our system. Which is making it more primitive and extreme.

At the networks, at the newspapers and magazines, they talk about this, the mad howl. Their staffers are subject to the personal attacks and ginned-up campaigns. They grab a mug of coffee, settle in on the set, lift the lid on the laptop, and the abuse pours out. It rattles them, as it would rattle anybody. Pressure groups string together whatever an anchor or correspondent has ever said on the air that is critical of their candidate. They produce a video of this, send it to network chiefs, and demand that the person be fired. They back this up with website campaigns: "Show your power, get this person canned." If the person they're targeting has, in fact, said equally critical things about their candidate's opponent, the sites and groups don't care. Too bad. The point is to show muscle.

Does all this make the targets of such campaigns rethink whatever views they hold, and change them? No. Why should it? But the sheer number of gross and furious messages, the glut of it leaves them wondering if the American people—their audience, the people they want to talk to, the citizens of the country they love!—haven't given themselves over, utterly, to rage.

(Perhaps you will say, here, that that's just too bad, you don't like the people on TV anyway; they're just a bunch of blow-dried blowhards. Fair enough, but when the bad time comes, in the first hours or days of it, they'll probably be the ones leading us through it. That's what happened on 9/11, when the president was in the plane and the vice president in the Situation Room. It was the network anchors and reporters who led us publicly, who gave us the data, told us the story as it was known, knocked down rumors. They were the heartening presence that day. They were great patriots. They will be again.)

To sum up: the anonymous posts of the Internet are what you'd hear if, in 1890, you put a megaphone in Bedlam and asked, "Would anyone like to say a few words?" Modern technology has empowered the unique and creative, but also the disturbed and destructive.

This too will have an impact on the '08 campaign.

So will this: the thirty-one-year-old campaign operative who's eager to make a name for himself as cunning and devious—really, they *want* to be known as dark—who's on the way up if only he can break through, and who replays in his mind over and over his own private version of *The War Room*, only this time the documentary stars not Carville and Begala, but him. In all his devious glory. He can't wait to play rough. He'll show the old guys how you kneecap the other guy in the modern media age. His area may be deep oppo, or slicing the base into pieces and figuring out which piece likes or hates which words and images, or slicing and dicing the other guy's base with tropes, rumor, and malice.

Watch out for him, for them. They're coming down the pike in both parties, and their work will not be pretty.

They could be stopped by grown-ups who know what time it is. And that may happen. We'll have to see.

The final and most serious part of the 2008 dynamic: For more and more Americans, politics has become a religion. It has become a faith. People find their meaning in it. They define themselves by their stands. And so it has become so very earnest, so almost existential. "I'm the kind of person who cares about AIDS in Africa." Or "I'm the sort who knows 'liberty' isn't just an abstraction." This becomes "I care about the poor and you don't." "You say you care about national defense but you really just love weapons and can't wait to use them." When politics becomes a religion, then simple disagreements become apostasies, heresies. And you know what we do with heretics.

There are many ways of explaining this, but I think it is what happens when government gets too big, when it occupies a large place in our lives. And our government is huge. When a government is big enough to intrude, to limit, with whatever legitimacy of intent, your autonomy, and more or less dictate many of your financial realities; when it is big enough to save suffering people on other continents and referee other nations' civil wars, and attempt to summon the resources to help all the disadvantaged, in whatever way they claim to be disadvantaged, then everyone gets into the scrum, some to defend themselves, some to protect their interests, some to encourage or redirect whatever good comes, or can come, from governmental power.

So: the facts make us partisans. And partisans can be bitter indeed.

All of this will be part of the background music of the 2008 campaign. So: it's probably gotten mean out there.

And of course it is not only the result of technology, and partisanship, and human mischief. Some of it has been the result of the past seven years, that trying time with which we have not fully come to grips. Some of the personalities and circumstances that shaped the era are about to ease off the stage. In some way we're about to turn the page. Maybe John McCain or Barack Obama can help us write something good on it.

A final thought on the longing to begin a new chapter that is almost palpable in our country. I was walking along Park Avenue one day this past July, a weekend afternoon, and passed by an old man sitting in a chair in the sun. He was on a little perching sort of chair in front of the grand building he lived in. This is unusual behavior on Park Avenue, and small though it is, it delighted me. You're allowed to sit in a chair in the sun on Dean Street in Brooklyn, but they're not so encouraging of such natural things here.

But there he was, and as I passed I smiled, he smiled, and I recognized him. A twentieth-century novelist, an artist, a man who's said true things. I'd met him once, years ago. So I stopped, told him of my admiration, and we talked. He is ninety now, had just had a series of operations, liked to come out here and read. There was an Edith Wharton novel in his hand, red cloth cover, yellowed pages. So we talked about Edith, and then he gave me a keen look. "Who are you for, the election? I guess the Republicans." I paused. "I haven't had to decide yet," I said. "I'm just watching and trying to figure it out. But I'll tell you, it would be a delight to me if Mr. Obama shows himself to be deep enough, sturdy and sophisticated enough that one could vote for him in good conscience."

His eyebrows shot up. "Oh, a lot of us feel like

that!" he said. With a real lilt, which is a beautiful thing to hear in a ninety-year-old.

I am a Reagan Republican. If John McCain shows enough seriousness and belief that one will be able to support him with conviction, that too will be a delight. But nothing is knee-jerk now. We need a renewed bipartisan spirit, a new openness to constructive ideas, whatever their provenance, and here is the thing behind my openness, and I suppose it won't surprise you if you've read this far: The age we live in is real, the challenges we face are real, and *before this is over we'll all be helping each other down the stairs.* The Democratic Party, a party with a great history that represents a significant portion of the country, at some point is going to have to become part of the leadership of the era. The time we are in isn't only half the country's story or a Republican story, it has got to be an American one, or we won't hold through it together. The only shield is a bipartisan shield. We must approach the world, to the extent we can, as one.

So I'll watch and figure it out like everyone else. People tell pollsters they know who they'll vote for, but I'm not sure they do. I think a lot of people are still thinking it through, and will decide as late in the game as they can. A great deal is in flux, with categories shifting and tumbling about. But it doesn't feel bad. There may be promise in it, or as much promise as history can hold while being what it always is, a bit of a tale of woe.

PART TWO

S ome thoughts on what was written on the page so many wish to turn.

What follows is a brief and mostly political attempt to come to grips with the Bush era.

The seven past years have been a hard time for our country, comparable in terms of stress and division to 1968, that killing year of war, riots, and death. And I think that in an odd way we both know this—know the Bush years have been difficult, and have changed us—and don't know it. We talk about it in the day-to-day, noting specific instances of damage, and of change. But I'm not sure we've come fully to terms with the era we've all just lived through. Maybe we only will when we look back on it, years from now, and give it a name. That's how it usually works, and in this case it's especially warranted, because the era began with an event that left us concussed.

There was a terrible day, 9/11, and in the shock of it we rallied together. It's still difficult for us to fully comprehend and capture what that day was. Three thousand dead. The Pentagon hit. The worst attack on American soil in our history. I'll never forget in New York, where we were rocked to our foundations, where the towers groaned and crashed to the ground, the rumor that started the night of the terrible day. "We may have lost fifty firemen." "No, one hundred, I heard!" "No, that couldn't be true." It was 343.

There's a story that captures some of the crazy shock of the first few days. It passed from parent to kid to parent. It was the story of the man who'd been on the 101st floor of the South Tower. He was standing at a window but he didn't jump, and when the tower began to come down a big metal beam came crashing by and he threw himself on it and held on for dear life. Down it tumbled, hitting updrafts of material and chunks of concrete, which broke at some points the speed of its descent. And he wound up on a heap of what had been the tenth floor and walked off alive. This is how crazy we were: we thought that might be true.

You know what it was like afterward: the flags, the million flowers at the doors of the firehouses. Everyone has different memories, something they saw, something said, but they're really all the same memory: something had cracked open our hearts and goodness came out, grace came out, and, as a fireman later put it, "altruism."

Everyone remembers the pictures of that day, but in the years that followed I thought more and more of the sounds. I always ask those who were there what they heard, partly because we've all seen the videotape and still pictures, but the sound equipment of the camera crews didn't really catch what people have described as the deep metallic roar.

Two years ago on TV there was a documentary about the ironworkers of New York's Local 40, whose members ran to the site when the towers were hit. They pitched in on rescue and then stayed for eight months to deconstruct a skyscraper some of them had helped build thirty-five years before. An ironworker named Jim Gaffney said, "My partner kept telling me the buildings are coming down and I'm saying 'no way.' Then we heard that noise that I will never forget. It was like a creaking, and then the next thing you felt the ground rumbling."

Rudy Giuliani said it was like an earthquake. My son, then a teenager in a high school across the river, heard the first plane go in at 8:45 a.m. It sounded, he said, like a heavy truck going hard over a big street grate at midnight.

But what I really found myself thinking about were the sounds that came from within the buildings and within the planes that hit them: the phone calls and messages left on answering machines, all the last things said to whoever was home. They still awe me, those messages.

Something terrible had happened, and life had been reduced to its essentials. Time was short. People said what mattered. It has been noted that there is no record of anyone calling to say, "I never liked you," or, "You hurt my feelings that time." No one negotiated past grievances or said, "Vote for Smith." Amazingly—or not, actually—there is no record of anyone damning the terrorists or saying, "I hate them."

No one said anything unneeded, extraneous, or small. Crisis is a great editor. When you read the transcripts that have been released over the years you can see it.

Flight 93 flight attendant CeeCee Lyles, thirty-three years old, in an answering-machine message to her husband: "Please tell my children that I love them very much. I'm sorry, baby. I wish I could see your face again."

Thirty-one-year-old Melissa Harrington, a California-based trade consultant at a meeting in the towers, called her father to say she loved him. Minutes later she left a message on the answering machine as her new husband slept, before dawn, in their San Francisco home. "Sean, it's me," she said. "I just wanted to let you know I love you."

Captain Walter Hynes of the New York Fire Department's Ladder 13 dialed home that morning as his rig left the firehouse at Eighty-fifth Street and Lexington Avenue. He was on his way downtown, he said in his message, and things were bad. "I don't know if we'll make it out. I want to tell you that I love you and I love the kids."

Firemen don't become firemen because they're pessimists. Imagine being a guy who feels in his gut he's going to his death, and he calls on the way to make things clear. Hynes's widow later told the Associated Press she'd played his message hundreds of times and made copies for their kids. "He was thinking about us in those final moments."

Elizabeth Rivas saw it that way, too. When her husband left for the World Trade Center that morning, she went to a Laundromat, where she heard the news on TV. She couldn't reach him by cell, and rushed home. He'd called at 9:02 and reached her daughter. The child reported, "He say, Mommy, he say he love you no matter what happens, he loves you." He never called again. Mrs. Rivas later said, "He tried to call me. He called me."

There was the amazing acceptance of extraordinary circumstances. I spoke a few years ago with a medical doctor who told me she'd seen many people die "with grace and acceptance." But the people on the planes didn't have time to accept, to reflect. They were in an immediate drama; they couldn't think things through. And yet so many showed the kind of grace you see in a hospice.

Peter Hanson, a passenger on United Airlines Flight 175, a dozy morning flight turned suddenly into a Higgins boat taking a hostile shore, called his father. "I think they intend to go to Chicago or someplace and fly into a building," he said. "Don't worry, Dad—if it happens, it will be very fast." On the same flight, Brian Sweeney called his wife, got the answering machine, and told her they'd been hijacked. "Hopefully I'll talk to you again, but if not, have a good life. I know I'll see you again someday."

There was Tom Burnett's famous call from United Flight 93. "We're all going to die, but three of us are going to do something," he told his wife, Deena. "I love you, honey."

These were people saying, essentially, "In spite of my imminent death, my thoughts are on you, and on love." I asked a psychiatrist once what he thought of this and he said he thought the people on the planes and in the towers were "accepting the inevitable" and taking care of "unfinished business." "At death's door people pass on a responsibility: 'Tell Billy I never stopped loving him and forgave him long ago.' 'Take care of Mom.' 'Pray for me, Father. Pray for me, I haven't been very good.'" They address what needs doing.

This reminded me of that moment when Todd Beamer of United 93 wound up praying on the phone with a woman he'd never met before, a Verizon Airfone supervisor named Lisa Jefferson. She said later that his tone was calm. It seemed as if they were "old friends," she later wrote. They said the Lord's Prayer together. "Our Father, who art in Heaven, hallowed be thy name . . ." And then he said those famous words: "Let's roll."

What I get from the messages is this: People are often stronger than they know, bigger, more gallant than they'd guess. And, of course, we're all lucky to be here today and able to say what needs saying. And maybe if you say it a lot it won't become common and so unheard, it will become known, and absorbed.

I came to think the sound of the last messages of 9/11, of what was said, will live as long in human history, and contain within them as much of human history, as any old metallic roar.

And that they could have been talking to all of us. "Hang in, love our country, take care of this beautiful thing we have."

That terrible day began in shock, and ended in unity.

But unity in a great nation of three hundred million, especially after such an event, is a delicate thing. It has to be treated delicately, almost reverently. It's not to be taken for granted, not to be assumed or abused. Its maintenance requires great care. And as we look back on the past seven years I think we have to say: it didn't get it.

We all know the geopolitical aspects of what followed. A great and wounded nation waited and then moved. A sharp strike into Afghanistan, whose government housed and helped Al Qaeda. The incredible charge of the horsemen of the Northern Alliance and the U.S. troops, together, against the Taliban forces. The toppling of that government. The hunt for Osama—get that man, bring him to justice, show the world, show the *young* of the world, "See what happens when you do such evil?" And show the world too, in our hurt, "See what happens when you attack this great nation? Don't. Tread. On. Me."

To have stopped at this point, in Afghanistan—digging in, strengthening, winning clearly and deeply, putting our resources into it and our concentration, coming to understand it, helping to turn it into a stable nation, building schools and hospitals, and continuing the crackdown on extremism; to have gotten Osama, dragged him from his cave; to have moved forcefully in all diplomatic realms and ways with a world full of friends. To have shown the world so much, to have done so much—.

It is sad to write that. It is painful.

Instead, we took a turn. I barely know anyone anymore, barely a single liberal or a single conservative, who would respond to the question "Did the president do the right thing when he moved on Iraq?" with the answer "Yes." And I live in New York, where a great many of the sophisticated liberals and even more of the experienced conservatives were persuaded, early on, that Iraq was the right thing to do. And the primary reason, always, was Saddam's possession of weapons of mass destruction, which he might funnel to terrorist groups.

So: another front, another war, the administration's insistence that we move before proof of the WMDs emerged in a mushroom cloud. The secretary of state, a sophisticated man never eager to commit U.S. forces, took the case to the UN and gave the evidence: broken promises, defiance of international agreements, satellite photos. Before that, I wasn't sure. After that, I supported the new war. Many Americans, I suspect, decided about then.

Debate was sharp, the 9/11 consensus was already beginning to fray—many of our allies weren't backing us, neighboring Arab states weren't with us—but these divisions were submerged in the first great burst of feeling that followed invasion: the seventeen days to Baghdad, the unstoppable Third ID, the toppling statue of Saddam. The relief that he didn't use poison gas on our troops, as he had on the Kurds. The liberation of the prisons where he'd abused dissenters, including children. There was a lot of tenderness those days, too: The first pain at the loss of American troops, the prayer chains for the boys who were there, and the girls too now. The deaths of the journalists David Bloom, that beautiful man, and Michael Kelly, that beautiful mind.

For a moment the war seemed all triumph, a terrible swift answer to what had been done to us on 9/11.

Then looting, insurgency, occupation, the long slog, no WMDs, no strategy, wrong strategy, IEDs, de-Baathification, years passing, tribal warfare, religious warfare, and the beginning, finally, of deep bitterness. The administration had bungled so much, so catastrophically. They didn't send enough soldiers, they didn't have a plan if things turned bad, they didn't know what they were up against, they thought shock and awe would turn old enmity into amity, and in their news conferences, they refused to acknowledge the depth of these problems, and their implications. They acted as if they were the most unserious thing you could be in a war: cocky, like a kid. I saw one of these, with Donald Rumsfeld, and then a news conference by the president, and I wrote of what concerned me, a sense of "mission inebriation." They acted sometimes as if they forgot that war is always—always—a tragedy. Sometimes needed, sometimes not, but always tragedy.

If this were a television documentary we would show here the USS *Lincoln*, May 1, 2003, and the S-3B jet zooming in, and the tailhook landing, and out steps the president in full flight suit, helmet in hand. The speech that followed, saying major combat operations in Iraq had ended, and the banner: MISSION ACCOMPLISHED. It wasn't, of course, not nearly, and that's why everyone remembers it, and Bush's foes love to use it. But I think of something else. When I first saw the ceremony on the *Lincoln* on television I was startled. Not disapproving—I assumed the bulk of the fighting was over, Baghdad taken, that some fighting would follow, but we'd be home soon, which is what I suspect a lot of people watching assumed—but taken aback. (People also assumed the *Lincoln* was in the waters off Iraq, when in fact it was floating off the coast of California.) No White House had ever done anything like this, the carrier landing, the president taking the stick, the Top Gun gear. I thought I was startled because I'd worked in an older White House, where our idea of a big event involved balloons, or remarks in China, Berlin, or on the coast of France. It took me time to realize that what was startling, and strange, was the *personalization* of it all—the idea that this victory was about *Bush*. But FDR didn't show up at Normandy on June 7 to make a speech; Reagan didn't fly over Grenada waving at the troops; that's not the way it's done, or ever should be done. It cast some doubt upon their judgment, both the president's and that of those around him.

I didn't realize for a while that the whole presentation on the *Lincoln*, the stunt of it, wasn't really modern, or, in terms of political communication, groundbreaking. It was, actually, a bit mad. Looking back, it signaled things about the attitude of the people making the decisions, or the nature of the forces behind them: they were pushing their luck, showing off, overstepping. It wasn't bold, it was careless. *They were looking for trouble.* But you don't have to look for trouble when you're president; it will find you. It knows your address. A White House is a castle surrounded by moats, and the moats are called trouble and the rains will come and the moats will rise.

It was as if they didn't know this.

*

Some of what went wrong is contained within an anecdote from David Boren, the former U.S. senator from Oklahoma, who during the first Gulf War, in 1990, was chairman of the Senate Intelligence Committee. (He would go on to become its longest serving chairman.) Boren, a Democrat, had backed the Gulf War. He had been impressed by the president's successful labors in building a broad, authentic, "not cosmetic" international coalition; he respected the administration's attention to the reaffirmation of the rule of law. When Iraq was booted from Kuwait, Boren quickly went to the White House to talk to President George H. W. Bush and his national security adviser, Brent Scowcroft, to tell them to finish the job. Boren bored in: U.S. troops should go on to Baghdad and remove Saddam. Bush and Scowcroft "forcefully disagreed." First they pressed Boren for his exit strategy. He admitted he didn't have one. From *A Letter to America*, Boren's recent memoir: "(Bush) and General Scowcroft then educated me about the longstanding division between the Kurds, Shiites, and Sunnis. They

PEGGY NOONAN

argued that Iraq would disintegrate into civil war, making it difficult for us to leave. Finally, they spoke of the balance of power in the Middle East and explained that the implosion of Iraq would tend only to strengthen the power of Iran . . . and place in greater jeopardy both Israel and moderate Arab states friendly to the United States."

Boren said that conversation, and others, changed his mind. He came to think the situation in Iraq didn't have "a purely American solution."

As president the past 13 years of the University of Oklahoma, Boren was writing in an attempt to tell his students what he'd learned of foreign policy. He summed up: regional realities, and a knowledge of history, must shape our decisions; we live in a multilateral, not a unilateral world, a unipolar one that is fast becoming multipolar; and we must act in concert with others, building coalitions, consulting our friends, and listening to them—just as Boren listened to Bush.

As the Iraq war wore on, I found the absence of this simple sort of wisdom hard to understand. So many who populated the second Bush administration were the experienced, stable Republican foreign policy establishment of the '80s: Cheney,

Rumsfeld, their top aides, sophisticated and in some cases brilliant men. What happened on 9/11 had left everyone concussed, and I believe the administration was sincere in its belief that Iraq had weapons of mass destruction. Those two facts changed things. But they did not suspend history.

History will have to explain what happened, but history can't do it alone. It needs first-person testimony—from the top. This process has been retarded in the past by what happens when individuals who were there speak about the inner thinking of the Bush administration. They beat your head in. But truly, the leaders of the war owe America—which gave them power and fame, which paid for their cars and staffs, which gave them life-and-death authority—the entire story of what and how they were thinking. They owe history the story, not books about how "On March 23, 2006, I sent a memo," but what was going through their heads, what data, arguments, personalities, and assumptions were driving them.

Abstract thinkers in Washington—and there were a lot of abstract thinkers at that point in Washington—were telling people far away in Iraq to do things, and were surprised when it didn't happen, and spoke, later, of their frustration. You'd shake your head. How could they be surprised? You don't flip a switch in Washington and things get better halfway around the world. There is something I used to think of after the first years of the war. It's a story of John F. Kennedy during the Cuban missile crisis. Tensions were high, a new sort of military diplomacy involving feints and a certain ambiguity was being attempted, and Kennedy didn't want any incidents that might make the situation hotter. He cautioned his generals: Get the word out to your men, no freelancing, no drama. He kept going back to it, and then shrugged, in explanation, "There's always some poor son of a bitch who doesn't get the word." He knew this because he'd been to war. He knew that it was by its very nature marked by chaos, disorganization, and miscommunications that always, somehow, affected the outcome.

Saddam was found in a hole in the ground, but where was Osama? Why was he still, two, three, four, five, six, and seven years later, on the anniversaries of 9/11, doing his videotape rants from a mountain somewhere? And then came the testimonies from the second tier of power, the presidential envoys and generals telling their part of the story, trying, understandably, to protect their reputations by explaining the context of their actions, but really saying, between the lines, that it was all ill thought through, all at odds with history, and that everyone was in charge (which was a problem) and no one was in charge (which was a problem, too).

Some good things happened. Our armed forces proved brave, determined, and up to whatever task they were put. They were the political heroes of the O's—as I think the decade will come to be known—the ones who showed endurance, who didn't talk but acted. And our country and media didn't make the mistake they had made thirty years before: no one stigmatized our troops this time; everyone, no matter their views on the war, respected them and showed it. This was a lesson from Vietnam. It's not true we learned nothing there.

And a big rethinking began, not in Washington but in your home and mine. The American people are not impatient, but they are practical. They were sacrificing in Iraq, and they weren't doing it to make things worse. It wasn't that the United States wasn't winning quickly. It was that three years in, the people of the United States couldn't even see a *path* to winning, a reasonable plan from the White House.

Three facts of this era seem now to be key to the fraying of our national unity.

One: In 2002 the Republicans had it all—the presidency, both houses of Congress, high approval ratings, a triumphant midterm election, early victory in Afghanistan. The administration had been daring and gutsy, but I think the string of victories left them with illusions about their own powers. It was all too heady, too triumphal. (In his recent book, *What Happened*, Scott McClellan bluntly admits the quick, deceptive victory in Afghanistan left them overconfident.) They were destabilized by good fortune. At this point they needed the calming hand of some wise old foxes, some group of Wise Men. (*Does Washington still have them? If they still exist, would anyone now listen to them? Would this White House have?*) They needed seasoned, case-hardened, worldly ones to come in and say, "Take a deep breath and slow down now, and think everything through. This big strong nation we've got is a delicate thing."

I remember the old fox Bob Strauss, former head of the Democratic National Committee, coming in during Iran-Contra to give advice to Ronald Reagan: *Settle down, get to the bottom of it, get the boat back on keel.* Reagan was the most successful president of modern times, but he knew when he needed help, and was not ashamed to ask. And if the giver of advice was a tough old Democrat, all the better.

Two: It was during 2002, when the administration was on top, when it had proved itself to itself—and it should be noted here that these were people who had been forced to flee the White House by foot on 9/11, that they'd been handed by history a terrible challenge, that they could not know, as human beings, that they would be able to meet it, and then seemed to themselves to be proving they were meeting it every day— that they should have been swept by a feeling of gratitude, and ascribed their triumphs not only to their own gifts and guts but to . . . well, let's leave it at a phrase like "higher forces," and the sacrifices of men and women in the field.

At that moment they should have reached out in an unprecedented way to the Democratic Party, included them in their counsels, created joint executive-congressional working groups that met often, shared the enjoyments of victory in Afghanistan, shared credit for it, thanked them for their support, been politically generous. This would have won for them—for the country—a world of good feeling, and helped the nation feel a greater peace with itself. Instead, in January 2002, barely four months after 9/11, Karl Rove went before an open meeting of the Republican National Committee, in Austin, Texas, and announced the GOP would use national security as a club against the Democrats. This marked the first deep tainting of the political atmosphere by a powerful figure, removing things from the patriotic level and putting them back down on the partisan.

Would the Democrats have been gracious in the same circumstance if they'd been in charge?

Oh my goodness, let's just agree the answer is, "Not all of them!" But that is not the right question. The right questions are: "What did America need after 9/11? What did the country need, a sense of good faith and unity at the top, or a weary knowledge that the old political warfare would once again commence?" Which, of course, it did. And never stopped, not to this day.

Three: The Democrats in Congress were, in general, unserious in their approach to the Iraq war, and not up to the era's demands. When the war was popular with the country they looked for ways to oppose it without political cost. But there's always cost. Thoughtful, tough, historically grounded opposition—and along with that, the need to answer the question "What exactly should we do rather than move on Saddam, what path should we take in the Mideast, and against terrorism; what is best now?"—would have taken a political toll; there was no way around it. When the war was less popular, and then unpopular, Democrats acted as if it were now, finally, a partisan issue that worked to their advantage. But it wasn't a partisan issue. America was on the line, America was on the *ground*. The Democrats in Congress weren't equal to the moment. They weren't equal to the best of their own history, either.

The fact is, both parties failed. This was well expressed in the end by Nebraska Republican senator Chuck Hagel, in January 2007, in a speech before the Foreign Relations Committee, when he spoke in favor of what was, essentially, a nonbinding announcement of no confidence in the administration's leadership in Iraq. He'd been under pressure after supporting the original Iraq resolution and then bucking the party, and on the day he spoke, without text or notes, he let it rip.

Congress, he said, had duties, and in the case of the war, meeting those duties had not been convenient, and so they had not met them.

"The Congress has stood in the shadow of this issue, Iraq, for four years. As [Senator John] Warner noted . . . we have a constitutional responsibility as well as a moral responsibility to this country, to the young men and women we ask to go fight and die and their families. . . . This is not a defeatist resolution, this is not a cut-and-run resolution, we're not talking about cutting off funds, not supporting the troops. This is a very real, responsible addressing of the most divisive issue in this country since Vietnam. Sure it's tough. Absolutely. And I think all 100 senators ought to be on the line on this. What do you believe? What are you willing to support? What do you think? Why are you elected? If you wanted a safe job, go sell shoes. This is a tough business. But is it any tougher, us having to take a tough vote, express ourselves . . . than what we're asking our young men and women to do? I don't think so."

Later: "I don't question the president's sincerity, his motivations in this. I never have. . . . Part of the problem that we have, I think, is because we didn't—we didn't involve the Congress in this when we should have. And I'm to blame. Every senator who's been here the last four years has to take some responsibility for that. But I will not sit here in this Congress of the United States at this important time for our country and in the world and not have something to say about this. . . . I don't ever want to look back and have the regret that I didn't have the courage and I didn't do what I could. . . . That is the essence of our responsibility. And if we're not willing to do it, we're not worthy to be seated right here. We fail our country. If we don't debate this . . . we are not worthy of our country."

Who came to fill the vacuum when the administration was flailing and not speaking frankly, and the Democrats were failing to come forward in intellectually coherent and therefore compelling opposition? Here I think is a central fact of the Bush years: a failed presidency, a failed Congress, and a mainstream media itself flailing and gasping for breath under its own pressures, allowed a new group to emerge to fill the thought vacuum. They were the Internet leaders, for the Net was old enough now to have leaders, who in turn had many followers, who sometimes, not always, moved crazily and en masse. From the left: *Bush lied, people died. The chimp started the war to pay off his corporate cronies.* From the lunatic fringe of the left: *9/11 was an inside job.*

The proprietor of the left-wing website Daily Kos captured the mood when he said, in April 2004, of four American contractors who were killed by insurgents in Fallujah, their bodies muti-

lated and hung from a bridge, "I feel nothing . . . Screw them." To his credit he soon took
the post down. But it is remembered because it
reflected the sound of the era.

On the right they busied themselves attack-
ing anyone who deviated from the administration's line. (And the line kept changing. We're
here because of WMDs. We're here because Saddam is Hitler. No, we're here to advance democracy. No, we're here because if we leave, genocide
will follow.) Soon they turned on each other. *You
don't support the war? Then you are not a patriot
and are banished from the rolls. Having doubts?
Why don't you just declare yourself a Democrat, for you're clearly not one of us. You criticize
Bush? Now, while we're at war? He's twice the
man Reagan was.* Reagan lacked courage, it was
explained, for pulling U.S. troops out of Lebanon
in 1983. Oh.

I had my own rounds in this arena when, after
years of arguing in support of Mr. Bush and his
policies in essays and columns in 2000 and after,
and taking time off from *The Wall Street Journal*
to volunteer for him during 2004, I listened to his
January 2005 inaugural address and found my-

self . . . disturbed. This wasn't an awkward president popping off in a press avail; this was a statement of purpose. Such speeches are prepared with deep care, and thought through for months. I wrote a piece for the *Journal* declaring the address to be what I thought it was: wild in its ambitions, immature in its thinking, and deeply ahistorical. Now I was treated as the enemy, too.

People said things had changed, the national debate had grown coarser. True enough, but what had really changed were not the harsh words or high passions of the era—both had marked our national political life from the beginning, and we'd more than survived. What was new was that the national political dialogue was moving, in the O's, from the less extreme venues of the past (the halls of Congress, the editorial board meeting, the letters-to-the-editor page, the solid if snoozy TV commentary) to a venue that rewarded and encouraged the primitive, the too-dramatic. The hotter the words, the more hits you got, and the more hits, the more power, and, it turned out, ad revenue. Nutty was good for business, a touch of nihilism even better.

All this contributed to an early sense of teamism that degenerated into gangism.

To be sure, as they say, the political websites offered a place to let off steam, and there's a lot of steam to be let off in a nation of three hundred million individualists. But they also helped inject a greater intemperance. (I should say here, because some in Washington like to dream up ways to control the Internet, that we don't need to "control" free speech, we need to control ourselves.)

To make it all just a bit worse, I think the Bush White House made a mistake that has not been fully noted. The political tactics that flourish within the new technology can come back to haunt. I think the president and his people were, as time passed, not fully confident of their case, and not sure that he was capable of making a sustained argument for his decisions, of taking hard questions and answering them. In part to make up for this lack, and in part to defend themselves from organized assaults from the left, I believe they mobilized the blogs, the cable shows, talk radio, the comment threads, and so on, to advance administration policy and to take down those who disagreed with it. But this uncorked a genie. In this atmosphere, Bush couldn't ever admit he'd made a mistake, on any issue at any time. He couldn't ask for assistance, couldn't show the kind of reflection about events that would have left voters secure in the knowledge that he was weighing things, aware of new data, alive to complexities. He couldn't even admit when he made changes of policy that made things better, when he took more moderate stances on foreign policy issues in the last years of his administration! It was all too polarized. They would have killed him if he had.

The forces the White House encouraged left it caught, with limited options, and stuck in the end with approval ratings at 30 percent or 27 percent, or whatever it is now as you read.

And all of this played out to some degree across the country, with the new acquaintance with the wrong views being hounded from the dinner table, and the couples who'd been close no longer speaking to each other. I remember when this happened last. It was when Vietnam turned bad.

✳

It seemed to me in the end that the Bush White House had come to mirror the thing they had hoped never to become, the Clinton White House, that in their essential natures and ways of operating the two had become alike, and that as such they constituted an actual break with the political culture of the immediate past. Both had an elaborate internal campaign and media structure; both treated day-to-day life as part of a permanent campaign; both had brutish impulses when opposed; both *personalized* the presidency in outsized and embarrassing ways. (Remember Bill Clinton walking, alone, through the halls leading to the podium where he was to speak at the 2000 Democratic National Convention, and claims as to his achievements—500 MILLION JOBS CREATED! WORLD PEACE ACHIEVED!—running as a scroll along the bottom of the screen? People laughed, and it was soon enough conceded by pretty much everyone involved that a shark had been jumped. But I suspect young Bush staffers, watching, thought, "That's the way to do it!") Both administrations were populated by too many individuals who were, essentially, just operatives, with the souls of lobbyists, which is what so many of them became.

The results of the 2008 primary campaigns were a comment on all this. The trope of dynasticism, the idea that there is something damaging and not right about two families digging in this way, that America is not a family-owned restaurant, that we are not helped as a nation at this time by—that we cannot *afford*—the hangers-on, hacks, friends, and courtiers who came to populate their governments, that we are not inspired by what they do to stay in power, spurred, I think, a good part of the national desire to say: Enough. Over. Turn the page.

Moreover, I think I correctly observed among many smart and accomplished adults in journalism and politics during the 2008 election the beginning of a hopeful shift. There came to be a certain convergence of views among people who hadn't agreed on much the past thirty years. To take a small example, leftist essayists in great liberal organs were expressing pretty much the same views as rightist essayists in conservative magazines on the issue of the continuance of Clintonism as embodied in Senator Clinton's presidential candidacy. (The most passionate people I knew who opposed Senator Clinton were not Republicans, they were Democrats.) It was a recoil against not only the notion of presidential dynasty but the ways of doing business, the specific methods of operation, of both dynastic organizations. I saw the new convergence as a sign of hope, indeed of democratic vitality.

Here is another truth of the past seven years, and again it took me time to feel I completely understood it. One cannot overstate the degree to which the Democrats had been traumatized as a party, as people, by the closeness of the 2000 election and the court decisions sealing the Republican victory. They felt it had been stolen. Less known is the degree to which Republicans too had been traumatized. I know I was. The 2000 drama was a wound to our democracy in that it diminished faith in the system, trust in the vote counting, and baseline respect among the members of each party for the other. There was suspicion, and assumptions of bad faith. I think this was the beginning of our latest great divide, the one that has given shape to our time and that 9/11, oddly enough, momentarily seemed to heal, or ease. But Iraq broke it open again, and broke it more deeply.

One of the reasons I came to see the administration's thinking as unwise was the context of the war, outlined above: it was an undertaking demanding of unity in a divided nation that had only recently—and tentatively—been reconciled by trauma.

As Jonathan Rauch noted in January 2008 in *The Atlantic* magazine, "In the annals of modern polling, the Iraq war has been unique in the degree to which it has split America along party lines." Rauch noted that while we think of Vietnam as controversial, it was actually more controversial *within* the two parties than between them. "The partisan gap in support for the war rarely exceeded 10 percentage points, and averaged closer to 5." Afghanistan was more or less similar. The Iraq war was different. By mid-2004, Rauch noted, "the difference between Democratic and Republican support for the war had reached *60 percentage points*" (my italics).

Here is a truth under which leaders of modern democracies must operate. What is possible matters. What is sustainable in terms of public support *matters*. Being able to persuade, to explain, to elucidate, and to lead truthfully, matters.

What happens at some future date if America truly *must* move—militarily, urgently, for its security, for the crucial protection of its strategic interests? After the past seven years, and in the coming years, it may prove hard, almost impossible, to marshal public support for necessary action. And this may carry grave implications for our country. In my time observing politics, since the late 1960s, Americans have often wondered if the Democratic Party was simply incapable of taking and holding strong foreign policy stands. Now they will wonder if the Republicans aren't too eager for engagement, too careless, too imprudent, too unsober.

One of the biggest political stories of the Bush era has been the Republican Party's squandering of its reputation for foreign policy sanity. It took fifty years to build it. More than fifty years. It is a tragedy to see it go.

✳

By 2007, in Washington, not enough people were playing the part of the adult, maintaining the good faith and good feeling that democracies, especially in the media age, need to flourish. Iraq was slipping away. It had reached the point where the administration couldn't even *define* what victory looked like.

And then a dramatic moment. The president, under pressure, had finally, earlier in the year, asked for more troops and appointed a new commander, who brought a new strategy. On September 11, 2007, the sixth anniversary of 9/11, Gen. David Petraeus, the commander of U.S. forces in Iraq, would appear before Congress to report on what the strategy was yielding.

It was a key moment. And in retrospect, a turning point.

It was clear before he spoke that the so-called surge of troops had gained at least some ground—decreases in the number of violent incidents, for instance. But it was clear as well that Capitol Hill wasn't eager to talk honestly about the situation. The air was sullen.

From the pro-war forces and those who supported the Iraq invasion from the beginning, what was needed was a new modesty, a willingness to admit things hadn't quite gone according to plan. A moral humility. Not meekness—great powers aren't helped by meekness—but maturity, and a shown respect for the convictions of others.

What the White House had been showing instead was the last refuge of the adolescent: defiance. Their attitude was "Oh yeah? We're Lincoln, you're McClellan. We care about the troops and you don't. We care about the good Iraqis who cast their lot with us. You'd just as soon they hang from the skids of the last helicopter off the embassy roof."

The administration and its friends were at that point being called thuggish. It was not unfair.

The antiwar forces, the "I was against it from the beginning" people, were, some of them, indulging in grim, and mindless, triumphalism. They showed a smirk of pleasure at bad news that has been brought by the other team. It was clear some of them had a terrible quaking fear that something good might happen in Iraq, that the situation might be redeemed. Their great interest was in seeing Bushism laid low and the president humiliated. They made lists of those who supported Iraq and who must be read out of polite society.

They had been called thuggish, too. And that also was fair.

At this point I was starting to feel that Washington was a city run by two rival gangs that had a great deal in common with each other, including an essential lack of interest in the well-being of the turf on which they fought.

Not only were hearts and minds invested in a particular stand, careers were, too. Candidates were invested in a position they took; people were dug in, caught. Every member of Congress was constrained by previous campaign promises: "We'll fight" or "We'll leave." The same was true for every opinion-spouter—every pundit, columnist, talk show host, editorialist, all of whom had a base, all of whom would pay a price for deviating from the party line, whatever the party and whatever the line.

And all of this was freezing things. It made

immobile what should have been fluid. It kept people from *thinking*.

What was needed was simple maturity, a vow to look to—to care about—America's interests in the long term, a commitment to look at the facts as they were and try to come to sober conclusions. That in turn would require a certain throwing off of preconceptions and previous statements. It required the mature ability to come to agreement with those you otherwise hate, and the guts to summon the help of, and admit you need the help of, the other side.

Without that, everything would remain divided, and our division would do nothing to help Iraq, or us.

It would have been good in the days before Petraeus's testimony to have seen the president calming the waters. Instead he upped the ante. A few days before Petraeus spoke the president went before the American Legion and heightened his language. Withdrawing U.S. forces from Iraq would leave the Middle East overrun by "forces of radicalism and extremism"; the region would be "dramatically transformed" in a way that could "imperil" both "the civilized World" and American security.

Here was the problem. Americans who opposed the war did not here understand the president to be saying, *Precipitous withdrawal will create a vacuum that will be filled by killing that will tip the world into darkness.* That's not what they heard.

This is what they heard: *I got you into this, I reaped the early rewards, I rubbed your noses in it, and now you have to save the situation.*

They felt a tight-jawed bitterness. They believed it was his job *not* to put America in a position in which its security was imperiled. They resented his invitation to share responsibility for the outcome of decisions they had opposed. And they resented it especially because he continued to grant them nothing—no previous wisdom, no good intent—beyond a few stray words here and there.

But there was another problem, and it was the biggest of all. *The president was right.* His essential warnings, at this point, were realistic. We couldn't just up and leave Iraq. Great nations can't just say, "Oops, I'm out of here." People were depending on us. They'd put their lives on the line for us. Our own soldiers had done that. A quick departure without thought to its vast implications would only have made it worse. And it was not in the interests of America or the world that it be allowed to get worse.

Would it have helped if the president had been graceful, humble, and asked for help? Yes. Would it have helped if he had credited those who opposed him at this point not only with good faith but with actual wisdom? Yes. And it certainly would have made news, for it would have been so unlike him.

The president's supporters couldn't summon grace from others because they'd so rarely showed it themselves. And grace and generosity of spirit not only would have helped, they would have provided the kind of backdrop General Petraeus deserved—the kind in which his words could be heard.

In the end, Petraeus reported to Congress, and he won the day almost immediately when the leftist website MoveOn.org came out with its famous "General Petraeus or General Betray Us?" ad. Talk about the extremes coming to affect the debate. They shot themselves in the foot and deserved to be known by their limp.

After the ad, Republicans enacted fury (*Thank you, O political gods, for showing the low nature of our foes!*), and Democrats felt it (*Embarrassed again by the loons!*). No one, no normal person, thought Petraeus was doing anything but trying desperately to save the situation for his country.

His testimony was dry, full of data points and graphs. He was earnest, unflappable, and low-key to the point of colorless. Maybe he thought things were colorful enough. He said the new surge of troops was working and could continue to work, and he won for the administration what it had asked for, more time. I felt relief that he didn't wear his heart on his sleeve or talk about our guys and gals in the field. He showed deep respect for them but didn't patronize.

But here was the great thing. He seemed like a grown-up. He was an adult doing a hard job with dignity.

At one point he was asked by Senator John Warner if the Iraq war had made America safer. And he didn't lie or spin. He said, "Sir, I don't know actually. I have not sat down and sorted it out in my own mind." Later, seeming to realize that his answer opened up whole new potential headlines that might have a negative impact on his immediate mission, he told Senator Evan Bayh that he'd been surprised by Senator Warner's question, and pointed out that "we have a very, very clear serious national interest" in Iraq.

There was another good thing: the level of sophistication and seriousness shown by Senators Barack Obama, Joe Biden, John McCain, and Chris Dodd, all of whom were running or were about to run for president, and who showed themselves equal to the moment. They were probing, occasionally strict, always respectful. It was a real relief.

From that point the situation on the ground in Iraq did seem to improve, and for that we must be grateful.

If progress continues, and a stable, sustainable government is erected, a prediction: Those who were wrong so long, who committed and then put in peril American blood, treasure, and prestige, will probably be what they've mostly been: smug. And their default position, triumphalist. And those who treated the war merely in partisan terms—and in the end, some of them hoped for the worst—will, faced with whatever progress eventually comes, probably be . . . blind. And their default position: change the subject. Might the Mideast, after all our efforts, wind up further stabilized? Let's hope. But let's not, this time, assume. For now we must make the best of it, learn from it—truly, *learn*—do nothing to bring greater turmoil, and leave when catastrophe will not follow departure.

But where did all this leave normal Americans? Not only Iraq and the four thousand Americans dead and the thirty thousand wounded and the trillion-dollar cost, but all the damaging political events of the O's—the psychic shock of Katrina, the immigration wars, gas prices, the faltering economy, the sheer weight, for everyone, of federal state, local, and sales taxes.

I think this, for a lot of people, for the vast life-upholding middle of the country, was more or less the arc: from shock, to a new engagement in our political life, to doubts, to disappointment, to feeling burned, and to feeling, in the end, a new detachment.

What's more, all this took place within a larger context of cultural change that was becoming more apparent each day. By the end of the O's, and especially during the 2008 campaign, I think a sense of who we are as a people was shifting. The presidential election was, among many other things, an epic encounter between the Old America and the New. To anyone over thirty-five or so they seem like—they are—different places.

Broadly, roughly:

In the Old America, love of country was natural. You breathed it in. In the New America, love of country is a decision, one you make after weighing the pros and cons. What you breathe in is skepticism and a heightened appreciation of the global view.

Old America: Tradition is a guide in human affairs. New America: Tradition is a challenge, a barrier, or a lovely antique.

The Old America had big families. You married and had children. Once, when I was interviewing Barbara Bush, she told me of the early days of her marriage, and out of my mind popped a question about why she'd had children. Her eyes widened. "Why, Peggy!" she said, and laughed me off. She meant: Listen, kid, you got married and had kids in those days, one followed the other, you didn't get all scientific.

Life happened to you. You didn't decide, it decided. Now it's all on you, it's all one discrete decison after another. It adds a particular weight. Old America, when life didn't work out: "Luck of the draw!" New America when life doesn't work: "I made bad choices!" Old America: "I had faith and trust." New America: "You had limited autonomy!"

Old America: "We've been here three generations." New America: "You're still here?"

Old America: We have to have a government, but that doesn't mean I have to love it. New America: We have to have a government and I am desperate to turn it into something I can love. Old America: Politics is a duty. New America: Politics is life.

Old America: Religion is good. New America: Religion is problematic. The Old: "Smoke 'em if you got 'em." The New: "Light that and I'll sue."

Senator McCain is, in his way, the Old world

of concepts like "personal honor," of a manliness that was a style of being, of an attachment to the fact of higher principles. Senator Obama is the New world, which is marked in part by doubt as to assumptions of the excellence of the old. It prizes ambivalence as proof of thoughtfulness, as evidence of a textured seriousness.

I weigh this in favor of the Old America. Hard not to, for I remember it, and its sterling virtues. Maybe if you are twenty-five years old, your sense of the Old and New is different. In the Old America they were not enlightened about race and sex; they accepted grim factory lines and couldn't even begin to imagine the Internet. Fair enough. But I do suspect the political playing out of a long-ongoing cultural and societal shift is part of the dynamic of 2008.

Not only Democrats and Republicans, and liberals and conservatives, were fighting it out, in venues both moderate and immoderate. The general breaking up of things spread to the Republican Party, where a great coalition, one built up over forty years with determination and love, was fall-

ing apart, sundered by various White House decisions, not only Iraq, and by a congressional
majority that had lost its way, and then lost its
majority. Republicans on the ground had become
concerned about illegal immigration—the number of those coming over the border illegally, the
implications of this in the age of terror, the cost,
the refusal of the federal establishment, the White
House and Congress, to take control. The president wanted what he called an omnibus bill—a
big and complicated bill that would rewrite most
aspects of immigration policy. It had support in
Congress, but not among the majority of Americans. On this, Democrats and Republicans on the
ground were in agreement.

At this point the American people were in
no mood to trust political proposals that were
complicated, highly technical, full of phased-in
elements and glide paths and Part Cs. They were
against complexity, not because they didn't think
life is complex. They know it's complex because
they live it every day. And they assume too that
public policy issues are naturally complicated.
But more and more they recoiled from complicated, lengthy, abstruse proposals because they

assumed—they knew—that professional politicians were using complications to obfuscate
and confuse. Voters assumed at this point that
politicians were using complexity to create great
clouds in which they could make an escape, like a
cartoon character, like Road Runner. Americans
don't trust "comprehensive plans," because they
no longer trust the comprehensive planners.

But what was most wounding, I think, was
that the president didn't really try to win over support for his plan by persuading, by speaking in
depth. Instead, he chose a form of verbal engagement that was crude, Iraq-like, and unhelpful. He
found it difficult to concede good faith on the
other side, to speak seriously of the legitimate
concerns of the bill's opponents. It was all fight-
fight-fight. The president took to suggesting its
opponents were unpatriotic—they "don't want to
do what's right for America." His ally Senator
Lindsey Graham said on television, "We're gonna
tell the bigots to shut up." Graham had gone on
Fox News and vowed to "push back." Homeland
Security secretary Michael Chertoff suggested opponents of the bill would prefer illegal immigrants
be killed. Commerce secretary Carlos Gutierrez

said those who opposed the bill want "mass deportation." Former Bush speechwriter Michael Gerson called those who opposed the omnibus plan "anti-immigrant" and suggested they suffered from "rage" and "national chauvinism."

How could they speak so insultingly, with such hostility, of opponents who were concerned citizens, and who were, often, though hardly exclusively, concerned conservatives, the president's own base? It was odd, but it was of a piece with a general governing style that was tearing the conservative coalition apart. Which sounds rather Beltway-ish, rather only-political, until you remember America is a center-right country. This was a lot of people who were being set against each other.

The White House and its supporters seemed to be marshalling not facts but sentiments, and self-aggrandizing ones at that. By the end I don't think they were even trying to influence the debate. I think they were trying only to lay down markers for history. Having lost the support of the country, they were looking to another horizon. The story they wanted written in the future was this: *Faced with the gathering forces of ethno-centric darkness, a hardy and idealistic crew stood firm and held high a candle of hope.* It will make a good chapter. Would that it were true! And why were they always so eager to turn normal Americans into the villain?

What was really driving both the Republicans and the Democrats, both party leaderships, on this, was, as always, mere gangism. "We'll get the Hispanic vote forever." "No, *we'll* get it forever!" What about America, and maintaining an air of peace and justice within it: Anyone interested in that?

The administration could have, if they'd really wanted to help things, created not one huge bill but a series of smaller bills, each of which would do one big, clear thing, the first being to gain control of the border.

Once that was done—actually and believably done, meaning voters would have to see it with their eyes, for they would no longer believe it only because their leaders told them it was true—the country would have relaxed in the knowledge that the situation was finally not day-by-day getting worse. They could begin to feel some confidence. And in that confidence, in that great sigh of relief, real progress could have begun.

Nothing radical was needed. We're not a radical nation. If only Washington had had some faith in this fact—and in *us*.

Most things can be worked out when there's good faith.

But in its absence . . .

And the Bush era was so marked by its absence.

How do so many of us feel now about our government, after what we've been through?

There are many ways to attempt to characterize it, but this may capture some of it. Think of where the vast middle of America intersects most embarrassingly, most infuriatingly, with its federal government. We are a nation of flyers. I travel an average amount, maybe more than some. I think my experience is probably fairly typical, because when I describe it to friends and acquaintances they often have similar stories, and worse.

Once, about two years ago, I flew to Florida and back to give a speech. This is what it was like.

9:30 a.m., West Palm Beach Airport. There are roughly a thousand people on line for the security check, all of them being yelled at by airport and TSA personnel. *Get your computers out. Shoes off. Jackets off. Miss, Miss, I told you, line four. No, line four.* So much yelling and tension, and all the travelers in slump-shouldered resignation and fear. The fingers of the man on line in front of me flutter with anxiety as he grabs at his back pocket for his wallet so the woman who checks ID will not snap at him or make him miss his flight.

After half an hour in line I get to the first security point.

Ahead of me, throwing bags in bins, is a young mother with a two- or three-year-old girl. The mother is tense, flustered. Bags, bottles, a stroller to break down and get on the conveyer belt. A security agent yelling: "Keep your boarding pass in your hand at all times." The little girl is looking up, anxious. All these yelling adults, and things being thrown. "My doll!" she says as her mother puts it quickly in a gray bin. "We'll get it on the other side!" says the mother. She grabs her daughter's hand roughly.

"Take off your sneakers!" a clerk yells.

The mother stops, hops, quickly removes her sneakers. Her daughter has already walked through the magnetometer and is wandering alone on the other side. She looks around: Where's Mommy?

Mommy gets her sneakers in a bin, on the belt, gets through the magnetometer.

I'm relieved. Her daughter holds her mother's leg. They begin to walk on.

A TSA clerk shouts to another, "You didn't check the sneakers. You have to put the sneakers through."

The second clerk yells, "Your daughter has to go through again!"

The little girl is scared—*What did I do wrong? I'm sorry, Mommy.*

The mother is tense, gets a look.

I lift my chin at the TSA agent, smile, and say softly, "Miss, that poor young woman with the child, she is having a tough time. The little girl is scared and—"

"We are following procedures!" said the TSA agent. Her mouth was twisted in anger.

I nodded and said softly, "I know, I'm just saying—a little gentle in your tone."

She looked at my ticket and smiled. "You have been chosen by the computer for extra attention."

"What?"

"You have been chosen by the computer for extra attention."

I get this a lot. I must be on a list of middle-aged Irish American women terrorists. I don't think most of us get extra screening because they think we are terrorists. I think we get it because they know we're not. They screen people who are not terrorists because it helps them pretend they are protecting us, in the same way, as Pascal once said, doctors in the Middle Ages used to wear tall hats: because they couldn't cure you.

Earlier I referred to how middle-aged women are treated under the new regime at airports, and here I wish to go on a little tear. Middle-aged women are the last gentlemen. They project the stature of life. They maintain dignity. They save the girl on the cell phone on the busy street as she chats away, ignoring traffic. She is chattering in the loud, somewhat grating accent of her generation, whose members tend to have the same sound wherever they come from, an accent formed in large part by TV, and reinforced by reality TV, but also in part by years of exotic orthodontia involving plastic, wire, and rubber bands. I believe it has left their jaw range limited, their speech both slurred and clipped, and because they've grown up with buds and plugs in their ears, being blasted by loud music, they, though they do not know it, often speak . . . loudly. (No one tells them this. But they are wonderful children, I know them and have taught them, and we must, for it is part of our job.) They are also used to living in other worlds in their heads, for many worlds have, in a lifetime of videos, CDs, and downloads, been implanted there. And there's the text-messaging.

So they are not always in the moment, not fully aware of their surroundings, not watching the traffic on the street, and they step off the corner while waiting for the light and fail to notice the car barreling right toward them, just fifty feet away and bearing down. Enter the middle-aged woman. Who is standing behind her, and who gently takes her arm—the girl allows herself to be directed, silently, like one used to being taken care of—and guides her back a step or two, and then says, as the car speeds by, "Sorry, didn't want you to get hit." And the girl blinks, nods . . . and continues chattering on the phone. That is the middle-aged woman. She is saving everyone. We don't want to lose her kind!

So keep this in mind as I speak of what it was like to be taken aside at the airport for what is called "extra attention" and "further screening" and was generally understood, thirty years ago, to be second-degree sexual assault.

I was directed, shoeless, into the little pen with the black plastic swinging door. A stranger approached, a tall woman with cropped burnt-orange hair. She looked in her forties. She was muscular, her biceps straining against a tight Transportation Security Administration T-shirt. She carried her wand like a billy club and issued curt instructions: *Face your baggage. Feet in the footmarks. Arms out. Fully out. Legs apart. Apart. I'm patting you down.*

It was like a 1950s women's prison movie. I got to be the girl from the streets who'd made a mistake. She was the matron doing intake. "Name's Veronica, but they call me Ron. Want a smoke?" She ran the wand over my body front and back. Beeps and bops, her index and middle fingers patting for explosives under the back and sides of my brassiere. More beeps, more pats. Then she walked wordlessly away. I looked around, slowly put down my arms, rearranged my body. For a moment I wanted to call out, "No kiss goodbye? No, 'I'll call'?" But TSA might not have been amused, and they're very unpleasant when they're not amused.

I experienced the search not only as an invasion of privacy, which it was, but as a denial or lowering of that delicate thing, dignity. The dignity of a middle-aged woman who has a right, actually, not to be mishandled.

Is this quaint, this claiming of such a right? If it is, a lot of us are quaint.

I got to my plane, settled in, took out my notebook, wrote my notes. I turned to the man next to me. "Did you have a bad time with Security?" His eyes got big and he shook his head. "It's terrible," he said, in an English accent.

He and his fiancée had come for a few days to

southern Florida; they'd been harassed coming and going. He said that he was a smoker, that he always carried a keepsake, a gold cigarette lighter he'd been given as a gift. Before he'd left for Florida he'd emptied it so it wouldn't light, and he showed it to the security people at the airport. They told him he couldn't take it on the flight. He asked them to send it to him; they said they couldn't, he'd have to go back to the ticket area and give it to them. But then he'd miss his flight. "It's your problem," they said. He wound up giving the lighter to an airline clerk. "An eight-hundred-dollar lighter! Empty!" He didn't know if he'd ever see it again. He said, "It's hard when"—and he put out his hands and shook them—"you're already a bit nervous about flying!"

I am certain the Englishman didn't come away from his experience with a greater respect or regard for our country.

But then, none of us comes away from the TSA with a greater respect or regard for our country, or its government. They treat us like cattle. And no one in Washington quite knows this, because no one in Washington wants to know it. Half of them feel this is what's got to be done in the new world; complain, and they look at you like you're soft, or don't fully understand the terrorist threat. The other side doesn't make an issue of it either. Maybe they think the more citizens are manhandled, the more likely they'll rebel, and throw the current bums out.

I think there is an unspoken subtext in our national political culture right now. In fact it's a subtext to our society. I think a lot of people are carrying around in their heads, unarticulated and even, in some cases, unnoticed, a sense that the wheels may be coming off the trolley and the trolley off the tracks, that in some deep and fundamental way things have broken down and can't be fixed, or won't be fixed anytime soon. That our pollsters are preoccupied with "right track" and "wrong track" but missing the number of people who think the answer to "How are things going in America?" is "Off the tracks and hurtling forward, toward an unknown destination."

I'm not talking about recent scandals, political campaign gaffes, or the ongoing election. I mean . . . the whole ball of wax. Everything. Geno-

cide, epidemics, nuts with nukes, crumbling infrastructure, a sense of unreality in our courts.
The fear of parents that their children will wind up
disturbed, and their souls actually imperiled, by
the popular culture in which we are raising them.
Senators who seem owned, actually owned, by an
interest group or financial entity. Great churches
that have lost a sense of mission, and of authority.
Do you have confidence in the CIA? The FBI? I
didn't think so.

But this doesn't quite get me to what I mean.
I mean I believe there's a general and amorphous
sense that things are broken and tough history is
coming.

Let me focus for a minute on the federal government, which has been, the past few years, another institution in trouble. In the past I have
been impatient with the argument that it's impossible now to be president, that it is impossible to
run the government of the United States successfully or even competently. I always thought that
an excuse of losers. I'd seen a successful presidency up close. It can be done.

But since 9/11, in the seven years after that
catastrophe, I have wondered if it hasn't all gotten

too big, too crucial, too many-fronted, too . . . impossible.

I refer to the sheer scope, speed, and urgency of the issues that go to a president's desk, to the impossibility of bureaucracy, to the array of impeding and antagonistic forces (the fifty-fifty nation, the mass media, the senators owned by the groups), and the need to have a fully informed understanding of, and position on, the most exotic issues, from avian flu to domestic tensions in Zimbabwe.

The special prosecutors, nuclear proliferation, wars and natural disasters, Iraq, stem cells, earthquakes, tort reform, did the FBI bungle the anthrax case, did you see this morning's Raw Threat File? What about Darfur? Our public schools don't work, and there's little refuge to be had in private schools, however pricey, in part because the young teachers who work in them are so embarrassed not to be working in the slums that they make up for it by putting up pictures of Frida Kahlo where Abe Lincoln used to be. Where is Osama? What's up with trademark infringement and intellectual capital? We need an answer on an amendment on homosexual marriage!

The range, depth, and complexity of these problems, the crucial nature of each, the speed with which they bombard the Oval Office and the Hill, and the psychic and practical impossibility of meeting and answering even the most urgent of them, is . . . overwhelming.

And that doesn't even get us to North Korea. And Russia. And China, and the Mideast.

You say we don't understand Africa? We don't understand Canada! We don't even understand Detroit.

Roiling history, daily dangers, big demands; a government that is itself too big and rolling in too much money and ever needing more to do the latest important, necessary, crucial thing. It's beyond "The president is overwhelmed." The entire government is overwhelmed.

And people sense when an institution is overwhelmed. Citizens know. If we had a major terrorist event tomorrow, half the country—more than half—would not completely trust the federal government to do what it has to do, would not trust it to tell the truth, would not trust it, period.

It should be noted that all modern presidents face a slew of issues, and none of them has felt in control of events but has instead felt controlled by them. JFK in one week faced the Soviets, civil rights, the Berlin Wall, and the southern Democratic mandarins of the U.S. Senate. He had to face Cuba, only ninety miles away, importing Russian missiles.

But the difference now, forty-five years later, is that there are a million Cubas, a new Cuba every week. It's all so much *more* so. And all increasingly crucial.

It will be for the next president, for McCain or Obama, too.

Sometime back I was chatting with friends about the sheer number of things parents now buy for teenage girls—bags and shoes tumbling out of the closet. When I was young we didn't wear earrings, but if we had, everyone would have had a pair or two. I know a twelve-year-old with dozens of pairs. They're thrown all over her desk and bureau. She's not rich, and the earrings are inexpensive, but her parents buy her more when she wants them. Someone said, "It's affluence," and someone else nodded. But I said, "Yeah, but it's also the fear parents have that we're at the end of something, and they want their kids to have good memories. They're buying them good memories, in this case the joy a kid feels right down to her stomach when the earrings are taken out of the case."

This, as you can imagine, stopped the flow of conversation for a moment.

And then it resumed, pleasant and free-flowing as ever. Human beings are resilient. We have to be.

A few years ago I was reading Christopher Lawford's lovely, candid remembrance of growing up in a particular time and place with a particular family, the Kennedys, circa roughly 1950–2000. It's called *Symptoms of Withdrawal*. At the end he describes a scene in which he, Ted Kennedy, and a few other family members had gathered one night and were having a drink in Mr. Lawford's mother's apartment in Manhattan. Teddy was expansive. If he hadn't gone into politics he would have been an opera singer, he told them, and visited small Italian villages and had pasta every day for lunch. "Singing at La Scala in front of three thousand people throwing flowers at you. Then going out for dinner and having more pasta."

Everyone was laughing. Then, writes Mr. Lawford, Teddy "took a long, slow gulp of his vodka and tonic, thought for a moment, and changed tack. 'I'm glad I'm not going to be around when you guys are my age.' I asked him why, and he said, 'Because when you guys are my age, the whole thing is going to fall apart.'"

Mr. Lawford continued, "The statement hung there, suspended in the realm of 'maybe we shouldn't go there.' Nobody wanted to touch it. After a few moments of heavy silence, my uncle moved on."

Lawford thought his uncle might be referring to their family—that it might "fall apart." But reading, one got the strong impression Teddy Kennedy was not talking about his family but about . . . the whole ball of wax, the impossible nature of everything, the realities so daunting it seems the very system is off the tracks.

Ted Kennedy has been in the United States Senate for forty-six years. He has seen a great deal, is an old lion, has canny personal judgments of those he's seen come and go, and as those who know him are well aware, he loves his country. He believes in his issues, and is by nature buoyant, optimistic.

And my thought as I read was: *If even Teddy knows . . .*

If I am right that such anxious thoughts are out there, and even prevalent, how are people dealing with them on a daily basis?

I think those who haven't noticed that we're living in a troubling time continue to operate each day with classic and constitutional American optimism intact.

I think some of those who have a sense we're in trouble are going through the motions, dealing with their own daily challenges.

And some—well, this part is about America's elites.

Our elites, our educated and successful professionals, are the ones who are supposed to dig us out and lead us. I refer specifically to the elites of journalism and politics, the elites of the Hill and Foggy Bottom and the agencies, the elites of our state capitals, the accomplished and successful of Washington and elsewhere. I have a nagging sense, and think I have accurately observed, that after 9/11, after its high feelings and fumbles, many of these people have made a separate peace. That they're living their lives and taking their pleasures and pursuing their agendas; that they're going forward each day with the knowledge, which they hold more securely and with greater reason than non-elites, that the wheels are off the trolley and the trolley's off the tracks, and with a conviction, a certainty, that there is nothing they can do about it.

So they've turned inward. They build new pools and plan exotic vacations. But have you seen their mansions in McLean? They're like little fortresses.

I suspect that history, including great historical novelists of the future, will look back and see that many of our elites simply decided to enjoy their lives while they waited for the next chapter of trouble. And that they consciously, or unconsciously, took grim comfort in this thought: I got mine.

Which is what the separate peace comes down to: "I got mine, you get yours."

You're a lobbyist or a senator or a cabinet official, you're an editor at a paper or a green-room schmoozer, you're a doctor or lawyer or Indian chief, and you're making your life a little fortress. That's what I think a lot of our elites, our business and political and media leaders, are up to.

Not all. There are a lot of people—I know them and so do you—trying to do work that helps, that can turn it around, that can make things better, that can save lives. They're trying to keep the boat afloat. Or, I should say, get the trolley back on the tracks.

And in this, though it would not occur to them, they are heroic.

By the end of the O's, the end of the Bush era, I think this could be said:

What began with love ended in dissension. The greatest political passions were funneled into opposition, not support. Democrats on the ground were left longing for change, and Republicans for Ronald Reagan.

At bottom, the bad political behavior of the era was a denial of the sincerity and meaning of 9/11. We meant never to forget it, and the warning it gave and the glory it showed, we meant to hold on to it and bring it into the future, and so many of us tried . . .

Here is what that day was, in its purest form, from Michael Daly's *The Book of Mychael*, which contains the best reporting to this date on the firemen's experience in the Twin Towers.

It's early, communications are down, the men don't know what's going on besides that a plane hit the tower and the fire up there is bad. All the men know is something is quite terrible about this thing, the bodies of the jumpers are exploding on the pavement, they can hear it, echoing like a series of booms, like a battle on some nearing shore. And the men of Ladder 5 and other companies are dragging their bunker gear—helmet, boots, oxygen tank, mask, fifty-six pounds of equipment even without tools or a length of hose—and making their way up the stairs to go save lives. They knew this was a rescue mission, that no one could put out the fire.

The stairway, Daly writes, was "only wide enough for a single file of firefighters going up and a single file of office workers coming down. . . . The office workers marveled at [the firemen's] spirit . . . the same spirit seemed to fill the office workers, who remained heroically calm amid this sudden horror, helping those who were burned and injured, calling out encouragement to the firefighters. The word Captain Jay Jonas of Ladder 6 would use to describe the prevailing emotion fit those going up and those coming down: 'Altruism.'"

That's who we fail with our mischief, our gamesmanship, our teamism, our me-ism.

And we of course must turn it around.

Because history isn't done with us yet. And America once again needs our protection.

PART III

S o: we have much to do.

I argue for a renewed sense of protectiveness toward America. Which means I argue for peace and preparedness: as much domestic and political peace as can be got within the confines of the knowledge that politics is a fight; as much preparedness as we can focus on without damaging our very American optimism, our faith that life is beautiful and full of splendor, and that in our attitude toward it we need not be, should not be, defensive, anxious, or dark.

We should set ourselves to reclaiming, to the extent we can, a bipartisan spirit that in the past yielded such glories as the Marshall Plan. We must try to reclaim our unity. We should leave behind bitterness and blame: they are empty wells. We must try again to be alive to what the people of our country really long for in our national life: forgiveness and grace, maturity and wisdom.

That's what I think people want. It's what I want.

Our political leaders will know our priorities only if we tell them, again and again, and if those priorities begin to show up in the polls.

I spoke earlier of the complexities presidents face, the entire federal bureaucracy faces.

For politicians, the serious ones, it is the same. We ask our senators and congressmen to make policy on: stem cell research, the Strategic Defense Initiative, NATO composition, the history and state of play of judicial and legislative actions regarding press freedoms, tax rates, the building of a library annex in Missoula, the most recent thinking on when human life begins, including the thinking of the theologians of antiquity on the point at which the soul enters the body, the Supreme Court, U.S.–North Korean relations, India-Pakistan relations, Securities Exchange Commission regulations, energy policy, environmental policy, global warming, progress in gender bias as suggested by comparisons of the number of girls who pursued college-track studies in American public high schools circa 1950 to those on a college track today, corporate outsourcing, the comparative efficacy of charter and magnet schools, fat levels in potato chips, national policy on the humanities, UN reform, and privacy law.

Luckily for us our congressmen and senators are smart as Einstein, virtuous as Mother Teresa, knowledgeable as Henry Kissinger plus Fareed Zakaria times Alexander Solzhenitsyn, and wise as Solomon.

Oh wait.

We have been asking a great deal of the mere mortals who lead us. And while we ask too much of them we keep them from doing—we allow them to avoid doing—the primary thing we need them to do well, which is know what time it is and act accordingly.

How do politicians themselves feel about all this? I would like to think many senators and congressmen, and I know some of them, sometimes go out and have a drink with friends and give vent to their surprise and dismay. *"I'm just a guy who loved politics! I buy my suits at Moe's Big and Tall! I'm not a theologian, I'm not a scientist! You shouldn't make me make these decisions! I'm stupider than you understand!"*

A year or two later they're still saying it: *"Look, I'm bright as the next guy but I'm not Socrates! Do you really want me to pretend I am?"*

But a lot of voters do seem to want them to pretend to higher wisdom than they possess.

Which leads politicians, after a few years in power, to the third stage of political bafflement: *"I just made American public policy on stem cell research, telling Harvard and Yale doctors what to do. Am I not Plato? Would you not like to kiss my hand?"*

This is the ego generated in people of whom impossible demands are made.

And the more ego-riddled they become, the less impressive they are, and the more we are put off by them. And wonder if anyone is really in charge.

They're a little hopeless. But they're what we've got! And in any case, senators have always been hopeless, and we've always muddled through.

With their areas of responsibility defined as the world, the universe, and the cosmos, it is no wonder that our politicians and network anchors—our most visible American leaders—tend to act as if they have attention deficit disorder. In their professions, attention deficit disorder is a plus.

What they need is a kind of political Ritalin.

What they need is focus. Provided by: us.

Most people have thought that at least since 9/11/01, the U.S. government has been focusing like a laser beam on issues of preparedness. But it is not. The past few years it has commissioned studies from every department of government on the reach and extent of potential devastation by a chemical, biological, or nuclear event. The streets of Washington are littered with them. But these studies are analogous to those done on what would happen if a category-four or -five hurricane hit New Orleans. We had plenty of studies telling us what would happen. Then it happened. And all plans and projections were more or less swept away in the drama that followed. And no one knew what to do.

✶

If I am correct that we are facing a hard time, and if deep in your heart you believe we're going to face a bad time, why don't all of us think about it a lot?

Because it's too big. Because we already went through a round of thinking dark thoughts after 9/11, and nothing happened, so maybe it's okay. Because terrorism has been hopelessly politicized as an issue. People, I think, feel that to warn, to prepare, and to ponder is akin to announcing they share and support a neoconservative vision of the world, in which war and antagonisms seem as much summoned as prepared for.

Because we know that we, individually, cannot solve the problem, and have to assume someone else will. Again, this is part of the division of labor, as we conceive it, between us and the federal government: I solve the problems I can solve (writing the tuition check, joining the school board), and the government takes care of the problems only *it* can solve, such as national and civil defense. But what if the people who populate our government do little each day about, say, civil defense, because, frankly, it has nothing to do with the current news cycle, which determines the daily office agenda? That is, it has nothing to do with the needs of the *NBC News* producer who just called asking the undersecretary for an interview on the latest stats on a spike in Social Security payouts. Social Security shows up in the polls. Health care shows up in the polls. "What Will We Do in the Next Terror Attack?" does not show up in the polls.

(Here I add a personal anecdote that is often on my mind. It was ten years ago, 1998, and I was having an informal lunch with a U.S. senator. The senator was a Democrat, and a great supporter of President Clinton. I got going on my fears on terrorism. I felt certain New York or Washington, perhaps both, was going to be hit by some bad people, and I assumed it would be a suitcase bomb, or a dirty bomb placed on a ship dragging through the harbor. None of what I said surprised him. But I pressed: You know Clinton. Why doesn't he begin to take extraordinary interest in civil defense now? I gestured toward the people in the busy Midtown restaurant. All these people are going to get hurt, I said. But if they look back and see that Clinton tried to help, that will be his great legacy. It's in his *interest* to do this! You don't understand, said the senator. What you're talking about doesn't show up in the polls. Bill Clinton will never do anything that doesn't show up in the polls! His candor took me aback. Not the content of what he said—that's how politicians are—but his blunt admission of the fact.)

Government workers are overwhelmed with the daily, the day-to-day, the bureaucratic and institutional distractions. They'll be as shocked as you when the bad thing comes.

But the biggest reason we don't think about the terror events we probably face is . . . it's a downer.

We elect presidents based on a number of qualities, including optimism—an optimism that they actually feel and we detect, or that they portray and we believe. We like them smiling and feeling good about the future and pointing toward newer, brighter horizons. They make promises within this context of optimism: they will lower taxes, freeing America of a burden, or raise

taxes, making America more equal; they will increase spending here or cut it there, start a great
new program or end an old unhelpful one. They
will be judged on these promises. Their legacy,
they believe, resides within them. So that is what
they try to focus on each day. (Along with the
usual in-box of surprises, both deeply consequen-
tial and not: Russia invaded Georgia; John Ed-
wards has a scandal.)

But the funny thing is, the next president's
legacy may well be—I think likely will be—determined by one thing: how he handles and leads us
through the next attack on America.

Which is something he never even talked
about during the campaign.

And by the way, if he had, if either Obama or
McCain had done a series of speeches saying we
have to prepare, he would not have been increas-
ing his chances of winning. "Obama Warns of
Doom, Recommends Existential Anxiety." If he'd
done that, he wouldn't have a chance right now,
would he? As for Senator McCain, from what I've
seen, the only reference his campaign has made
to a future domestic terror event is top aide Charlie Black's statement to a *Fortune* magazine re-

porter in July 2008 that if there is a terror attack before the presidential election it will probably redound in the Republican's favor. He was roundly condemned for this. But all I thought when I read it was, "Thank you, Charlie Black, for revealing how the people who run America really see these things, as events of deep partisan import!"

But if I am right—and if you are right, too, for if you've read this far you're probably to some extent in agreement—that something big and bad is going to happen to America, that we're going to get hit again, and that before the era is over we'll all be helping each other down the stairs, then certain things follow.

What I offer here is not a fourteen-point program. I speak broadly, not comprehensively or technically. What follows is not a government study featuring such sentences as "Critical infrastructure protection requires triple-tiered response initiatives including but not limited to the efforts of multiple private-sector entities operating with and in conformance to federal, state, and local quality-control efforts." Believe me, I've read these reports. You don't ever want to read them. They are marvelous collections of wordage—they are mass word-dumps—that seem actually designed to tell you: nothing.

So, some rough thoughts on what I think we need.

We need the best possible national defense, coupled with an attitude of wisdom, forbearance, and peacefulness toward the world. A civil defense system worthy of the name. An America that is stronger at home—with a stronger physical and cultural infrastructure. A new civility, or rather a new regard and affection within our political culture, based on the fact that we know a unique challenge is coming, that it may be soon, and that we will have to get through it together.

Here are some thoughts in connection with the above.

If I am right, then—as I've said—what we need most right now in our national political life is a kind of patriotic grace, a grace that takes the long view, apprehends the moment we're in, comes up with ways of dealing with it, and eschews the politically cheap and manipulative.

What does this mean in practice? It means, to begin with, that we must change not only the substance but the tenor of our political discourse. I am not referring here to the things "political strategists" say on cable talk shows. It's not the bickering on TV that is the problem. (And they don't even bicker all that much; they just bark their talking points and then go to dinner at the Palm.) This is only an expression of the problem, and in any case is not harmful because it excites only those who are already polarized. Everyone knows TV's cable show performance artists are in essence paid to take a side and stick with it no matter what. Did you ever see one of them look away for a moment and then say, thoughtfully, that their party was wrong on some great issue, or not facing a problem, or playing with it for gain? I don't think you have. They're hired to do what they do, and sophisticated people—the people watching the news-talk-political shows—know this.

It is not the bickering that's important; it is the spirit behind the bickering.

It is a spirit of mindlessness. It is a spirit that says, "You know the general tranquility we enjoy?

It will continue forever, so we can play our little games within it forever." It is a spirit not of optimism but of dim, conceited carelessness. It was an understandable spirit when America was fat, happy, and under no direct and immediate threat. But it doesn't fit the needs of this age.

What is more important, more deadly, is what political professionals do to advance the cause of the candidates who employ them. These people divide us cynically, needlessly, for small and temporary partisan gain. It is too late for—we no longer have time for—the old ugliness. Once, perhaps, we could afford it. Once, the stakes were not so high.

There is a thing among political enthusiasts of the right and left: they care. They care so much they allow it to make them ugly. They use their honest concern—and on some level most of them feel some honest concern for something, some issue—to rationalize cruelty to the other side. This is human, and understandable. But . . . they shouldn't be rewarded for it.

Powerful interest groups and political action groups are part of the problem. They pursue their issues as if there is no other issue in the world;

they act as if they care about nothing but pushing the agenda they are so well paid to push. They are national, Washington based, and have the financial clout to bring senators and congressmen to heel. They are the original "separate peace" people; it's always the fat 1990s for them. Only it isn't the '90s anymore.

This is no time to stop the national political debate. Conservatives are certain as to the rightness of their general philosophy, or one should say their understanding of the world. I share it. The left is certain of its rightness also. Fine. Let each side hold high the banner and make its case. But the tearing apart of the country to win, the manipulating voters you don't even respect to triumph, the making America worse to get what you want . . . that will not do.

That is yesterday. It is over. Stop it.

Also: If the time we are living in is so high-stakes, shouldn't we be discussing this in our elections? Here is a suggestion for one of the presidential debates. "Senator, if, one day during the beginning of your presidency, there is a great flash in Washington, and then the sound of explosion and wreckage, what are the first things you will do? That is, once ensconced deep down in the bunker that will become the Situation Room, and given information as to the exact nature of the event—a nuclear explosion—what actions on your part will follow? Do you know at this time what can and will be done to help the populace of the greater Washington area survive? Do you have a plan to deal with the fact that it might be weeks or months before we know exactly who, what group or actor, attacked us? Can you tell us how you will direct armed forces to proceed both locally and internationally? And did you consider this scenario, sir, when you were deciding to run for the presidency?"

That would be a good place to start.

If I am right, those things that *ease* the stresses we feel as a nation, the tears and divisions we feel, should be encouraged. We drive each other crazy. We array ourselves in groups and announce our grievances, demanding that other groups respond and address them. We fight as if we'll never need each other. We fight like a crazy drunken family hurling charges against each other in the living room while there's a fire in the attic and it's travel-ing down the stairs. Well, I think I'll stop here. You get my point.

One example, out of a thousand one could choose:

We have spent the past few years tearing our-selves apart over immigration. We didn't have to; we don't have to. Why not be humane, be Ameri-can, and recognize the moment we're in? Take a pause, close the border to illegal passage now, for reasons of national security. Continue legal im-migration, with an eye to one thing: admitting as new citizens those who bring particular skills our nation particularly needs.

As for those who've come here over the past twenty years or so illegally . . . easy does it. There, that's a platform for the moment: *Easy does it.* Some of the immigrants now in America illegally came in because the door was open. (The federal government kept it open, cynically and in a bully-ing manner, and for this deserves continued criti-cism.) Those who break our laws, indulging in violent behavior? Send them back. Goodbye. Those who join our armed forces and become part of our national defense? Grant them citizenship, with the thanks of a grateful nation. Those who peacefully contribute? *Easy does it.* Let what is, be. Close the border for now but allow the law-abiding who remain among us to become Americans. *Help them to come to see themselves as Americans.* (More on this in a moment.)

If I am right, then things that encourage our cohesion as a nation should also be passionately supported, and spoken of in a new way, with a new urgency.

We really must tend to the ties that hold us together as citizens of America. These ties have gotten thinner, more frayed, in our lifetimes.

Here is one thing that holds us together, if we let it: Our history. A sense that we have inherited and are part of a great nation created by men and women whose lives still have much to teach us, whose lives can move us, can electrify our intellectual environment and help us see ourselves more clearly. The young of our country—and, again, our newest Americans, members of the great wave of immigrants of the past twenty-five or so years—need to know *they are part of a con-*

tinuum, a human continuum of great meaning and worth. If they are taught a love of country it will help them respect themselves—it will help them to know they are connected to that, they are part of that, they are another expression of the continuum. In a crunch—in a terrible moment of history—we will benefit from a renewed patriotic sense, and thank ourselves for having encouraged it. A shared sense of pride in who we are and what we've been will help us see each other as . . . the same. That sameness will be a real glue in a tearing time.

Part of what I'm saying has been said, better, by Bruce Cole, the head of the National Endowment for the Humanities, in a speech at New York University in the summer of 2002. He warned of "American amnesia," noted a study of students at 55 elite universities that found over a third couldn't identify the U.S. Constitution as establishing the division of powers in our government; 40 percent couldn't place the American Civil War in the correct half century; and two-thirds didn't know what the word "Reconstruction" referred to. "Citizens kept ignorant of their history are robbed of the richness of their heritage. . . . A nation that does not know why it exists, or what it stands for, cannot be expected to long endure. . . . We cannot expect that a nation which has lost its memory will keep its vision."

But another part of what I'm saying is that we have to teach our history with more love.

In our schools, the deadening history textbooks our children are forced to read, with their leaden prose and utter lack of aliveness to life, to its depth and meaning, tend to remove the person from history. It's all big abstract forces. But history is human. And it is not only a long tale of woe.

As a society, we have attempted over the past fifty years to correct and rebalance the Parson Weems-ish hagiography of the past, with the perfectly virtuous young George Washington bravely refusing to deny that he'd cut down the cherry tree. That's good, we needed to. The story of America is not one sweet thing after another. But we have overcorrected; we have lost balance and tipped into the unnecessarily—and unrealistically—negative. It's not good for our kids. It doesn't make them stronger. It doesn't leave them with something proud to share. It won't help them hold together in a difficult time.

And this is true not only in our schools, but in our culture. I was talking to a journalist recently about the impact the movies have made the past eighty years on America's conception of itself. I told him of one huge way they'd made an impact on me. The old buccaneers who invented Hollywood and who ran it in the 1930s and '40s somehow always portrayed Irish Americans, and Irish Catholics, as pretty wonderful people— daring and beautiful and funny and brave. I am grateful that they did this! Because it helped give me a conception of my own people. So many movies now are so unrelievedly dark that it's hard for them to . . . celebrate anyone. It's a world without heroes, they think, so why would the new Russian immigrant to America be a hero, and be portrayed as one? But maybe the new Russian immigrant needs what I needed: a sense that I was part of something beautiful.

Great cultures can always afford darkness when everything's safe, secure, and rich. They need something more nourishing when things are not.

Here is another area with room for improvement, though I don't have a clue how to get it. During the past seven years the end of the old media monopoly—the end of the big three networks and their big three news broadcasts—came to play an important role in our national life. And again, this is something we've both noticed and not noticed. It was all so gradual, we acclimated ourselves, and enjoyed more choice.

But the breakdown of the old mainstream media was not, is not, all to the good.

During the past decade we made much of the freeness of new media produced by technological advancement. We love its wonderful barbaric yawp. But it's also true that the old essential unity one used to experience when one turned on the TV in 1970 or '80 has been fractured, broken up. And we ought to pay more attention to this, because . . . we don't want to get too balkanized and ghettoized, and niched.

Conservatives see what has happened as essentially good: more freedom. Liberals, less so. (I think it an odd thing about modern liberals that they're made anxious by the unsanctioned. I thought the liberal spirit was an essentially artistic one, and the artistic spirit loves boundary-breaking.) I know that they feel the old impartiality of the broadcast news of the Big Three past has lost its place of respect; I know conservatives answer, rightly in my view, that the impartiality of the past wasn't really so impartial.

It is good when information monopolies fall. But there are downsides, and I think all of that, all of this changing in the media world of TV, had an impact on how we all viewed—literally how we all *experienced*—the past seven years.

We're not sharing the same information anymore. We used to share the same information—and argue about it. But now more and more we don't even get the same essential facts, or headlines. And I think in part this change had an impact on how we actually viewed the political realities of the past seven years. If you wanted to hear that Iraq was a great success, you went to Fox. If you wanted to hear that the generals in the

Pentagon were rebelling against White House leadership, you went to CNN. If you wanted to take a full, deep bath in George Bush's greatness, you went straight to one cable show; if you wanted all the arguments on the enormity of his failures, you went to another.

I know this is freedom, or some approximation of freedom.

But I can't help but think there's something disconcerting, and not all good, with not sharing roughly the same data anymore. Even in the old days of major broadcast network bias, the bias could go only so far. It was inhibited by certain limits.

The O's had no limits. And no boundaries either. Yet the truth seemed as elusive as ever.

This sort of thing is never a problem or a challenge for the sophisticated and mature. But it causes problems for . . . well, for those who cannot think easily or well.

Is there an answer? I don't know, the genie's out of the bottle. But I'll tell you: twenty-five years ago, chafing at what I believed and believe was the bland corporate liberalism of the news pages of the great newspaper broadsheets, I hoped America would become more like the British model: If you wanted "conservative news" you went to the *Telegraph*; if you were a liberal and desired a daily injection of its worldview, you read *The Guardian*. That's more or less what we have now. So it's funny I find myself rooting, now, for the survival of the dying broadsheets, and the clout-losing Big Three news programs. They enforced, however imperfectly, a certain professionalism, certain rules of the craft, certain boundaries. And boundaries aren't all bad. That's why there are walls around mental institutions.

More than that, because the big three networks and establishment broadsheets were the only game in town, they felt required to do some things that the million channels and billion blogs do not feel the responsibility to do. They covered big stories in depth, committing hundreds of reporters and producers to coverage. Twenty years ago the big networks sent three to four hundred people to cover a national political convention top to bottom. There was barely a delegate in a funny hat who wasn't interviewed. They even covered, in their lame and sometimes biased ways, but covered, the creation of party platforms.

The big networks this year will each send maybe a hundred staffers to each convention. And they'll show only parts of the conventions, one or two hours a night. Why do I think this isn't progress? Maybe in part because I haven't seen a single story this year on the preparation of either party's platform.

All big changes have unexpected benefits and un-anticipated drawbacks, and here is another: the loss of the man on the train.

Forty and fifty years ago, mainstream liberal media executives—middle-aged men who fought at Tarawa or Chosin, went to Cornell, and sat next to the man in the gray flannel suit on the train to the city, who hoisted a few in the bar car, and got off at Greenwich or Cos Cob, Conn.— those great old liberals, had some great things in them.

One was a high-minded interest in imposing certain standards of culture on the American people. They actually took it as part of their mission to elevate the country.

And from this came . . . *Omnibus.*

When I was a child of eight or so I looked up

at the TV one day and saw a man cry, "My horse, my horse, my kingdom for a horse!" He was on a field of battle, surrounded by mud and loss, and I was riveted. Later a man came on the screen and said, "Thank you for watching Shakespeare's *Richard III*."

And I thought, as a little American child: That was something. I gotta find out what a Shakespeare is.

I got that from *Omnibus*. And I got *Omnibus* from those old men on the train.

They were strangers, but in the modern media era a stranger can change your life.

And because the men on the train had one boss, who shared their vision—a William Paley, for instance, who owned CBS, and who didn't want his legacy to be *My Mother the Car*—and because the networks then had limited competition, and the pressure to live or die by ratings was not as intense as it is today, they could afford an indulgence. Also, and not insignificantly, the government actually pressed them to afford such indulgences.

The result was a lot of programming that was a real public service.

Now the man on the train is a relic, and no one in the networks is saying, "As the lucky holders of a broadcast license we have a responsibility to pass on the jewels of our civilization to the young." To say that now, in a competitive network environment, would be saying, "Please, please give me a ticket to corporate oblivion!"

TV is still great, in many ways better than ever. My own life was enhanced throughout the O's by *The Sopranos*, *The Wire*, by the old *ER*, by *30 Rock*, so many great shows. *But when we deposed the man on the train it wasn't all gain.* And we can all sit around saying it's great that no longer can the old liberals impose their vision, but what has taken its place, often, is programming for the lowest common denominator.

I spoke about two years ago with a network producer, an old warhorse who was trying to explain his frustration at the current ratings race. He wrestled around the subject, and I leaned in with blunt words.

"You mean it's gone from the dictatorship of a liberal elite to the dictatorship of the retarded," I said.

"Yes," he said.

And that's not progress.

When liberals miss something in the media, that's what they should be missing, the old standards. When conservatives say there's nothing to miss, they're wrong. We lost a world of bias, but we lost some elevation, too.

And you know what? Our kids need it. Our new Americans need it. Shakespeare can do a lot to keep a people together.

If I am right, American foreign policy should pick itself up, dust itself off, and start all over again. We have lost some of our standing in the world. We have lost some of our authority. We have lost some of our friends.

To begin with, we should be careful not to make the world a hotter, more discordant place. It is quite hot enough. We should go to great effort to proceed with calm, wisdom, and maturity. We should nurture our friendships, and find new ones. We might be guided by these words, from our Declaration of Independence: "a decent respect to the opinions of mankind . . ."

We need friends in the world. This is never

easy, will never be perfectly achievable, and never has been in the history of man. Different nationalities tend to view each other, even in the absence of any particular reason for hostility, as: The Other. And we are in a very particular position, as the most powerful nation on earth and, by many measures, the wealthiest. This gives us a special challenge.

The wealthiest, most influential, and well-connected family in your old town when you were a kid: Did you love them up there in their big house? When they attempted to have their way in the city council, even when they were right—maybe even especially when they were right—did you always feel unalloyed pleasure when they succeeded? Or did you, perhaps, hold mixed feelings, or harbor resentments? When tragedy befell them, were you ashamed to detect within your breast some unbidden twitch of . . . delight? That is how human beings are. That is how nations are.

Good advice for the richest family in town: Don't lord it over people. Be who you are and then better: humble, gracious, authentically interested in not only your neighbors' views and problems but their *reasons*. Help when you can.

• • •

Here is a very small example of how obnoxious we can seem.

This is from a Sunday morning blog post by the writer Jim Manzi, on the pro-Bush *National Review* Online. "So here I am spending a Sunday afternoon in London's Heathrow Airport, as I have on far too many Sundays in my life. It turns out this visit will be quite a bit longer than normal, thanks to President Bush. He landed here a few hours ago, shutting down the airspace of one of the world's busiest airports. They are now working through the delays, largely by cancelling numerous flights throughout Europe. There have been pretty acid press descriptions of the President's airborne baggage train: Air Force One, a full back-up 747, a 757, and four helicopters. And that's in a very pro-American paper. There were significant delays on Thursday here as various armored cars were pre-positioned. Yesterday multiple helicopters did a series of practice exercises for today's landings that apparently created multi-hour delays as well. I sure am glad we don't act like an empire."

He continued. "Place yourself in the position

of a middle manager at Sainsbury's getting a flight to Amsterdam, who is now spending an extra four to seven hours in the airport—if he's lucky enough to get to Amsterdam at all tonight to make his meeting tomorrow morning. A harassed gate agent explains why this delay is happening. Multiply by about 100,000. You can't imagine just how much goodwill has been created for the U.S. here at this airport today.

"Really, who would like this country? This is not the GI's who came to liberate France and were grateful for a cup of water; this is the world's superpower come to make your life more difficult."

This struck me as a small but beautiful example of the impression we make, wholly innocently, if it can be called innocent to act in a way that takes no account of the fact that others share your airspace.

The answer is not "The president should never go anywhere." The answer is to consider whether this empire-like security, which looks so defensive, so frightened, so "We know you're trying to kill us"—can't be made less intrusive, insistent, and bullying. We treat our presidents now as if they were the Great Untouchable Caesar-

Pope of the Chrysanthemum Throne. When, actually, they're the guy we hired for four years to be chief executive, and soon he'll be replaced. The system was not built to be Caesaric. *We* were not built to be Caesaric. We should settle down.

One of the things we will have to do this election year is consider what American foreign policy should be in the future.

We will have to consider what challenges we face, what is needed from America, and for her. In some rough and tentative way we will signal where we stand regarding what philosophical understanding of our national purpose rightly guides us.

I've always believed "isolationism" to be a canard, that we are not and never have been an isolationist country.

Our people came from every country on earth and held fierce opinions on the political realities of the nations whence they came, and the nations that had helped and hindered those nations along the way.

Here's something every American is born with: his own foreign policy. If you were an Irish

American born in 1900 in Boston you learned quickly enough at the kitchen table that "we don't like the English," and you probably absorbed some of this animosity even though you'd never met an Englishman and, actually, the English are America's oldest friends, and you're an American. It's complicated. It's always been complicated. The Italian woman down the street said to keep away from Sicilians; Jews from Russia said watch out for that nation. My old friend, an Armenian, often informed me that America should never support his family's old foes, the Turks.

The immigrants to America in the twentieth century spent half their time sending money back to the home country. You might say they were working to keep their old countries afloat. This wasn't very isolationist of them—of us. The immigrants to America of the twenty-first century? They do the same. That isn't very isolationist either.

In Europe the nations are all bundled up together; of course the Germans vacationed in Italy, and came to know it. America was a vast continent; there was only itself from one ocean to the other; in between were pieces of America, states and cities and regions; it was enough of a project for us just to push west; it was exotic enough to make stops along the way. You could discover whole new cultures! In Chicago they had their own accent, just like the other American cities, and their own phrases. You had to listen to learn. The South had one culture, the West another, New England another. We didn't have to leave America to travel broadly.

Did we enjoy fighting the wars of one nation an ocean away in a territorial dispute with another nation an ocean away? No. Why would we? The great powers of Europe didn't decide the outcome of our Civil War by taking sides and deploying troops. Why would we have done it to them? And yet twice we crossed the Atlantic to idealistically fight and die in Europe's wars. And won both. And took no territory.

This they call isolationism? How about We-Were-Modest-and-Minded-Our-Own-Business-Because-We-Had-a-Lot-of-Business-to-Handle-But-Came-in-to-Help-When-We-Thought-It-Wise-and-Decent-ism.

Anyway, the argument isn't about isolationism.

A good part of the current debate will be shaped by the tugging back and forth of two different schools of thought, two different attitudes. There are those whose impulses are essentially interventionist—we are the great activist nation, the spreader of political liberty, the superpower whose meaning is made clear in action. And it's good to pass very public judgment on the awful ways of all other nations; it helps them reform.

The other school holds profound reservations about this. It is more modest in its ambitions, more cool-eyed about human nature and history. It feels more bound by the old advice attributed to one of the Founding Generation, that we be the friend of liberty everywhere but the guarantor only of our own. We must not roam the world looking for monsters to slay, said old John Adams. Who added that if we do, we will lose who we are.

Much has changed in the more than two centuries since he said it: many wars fought, treaties made, alliances forged. And yet as simple human wisdom, it packs a wallop still.

Those who tug toward the old Founding wisdom—I am one—often use the word "beacon."

It is our place in the scheme of things, it is our fate and duty, to be a beacon of liberty. To stand tall, to hold high the light. To be an example, an inspiration. "See what America is—let's try to be like that." We do not invent constitutions and impose them on other countries; instead they, in their restlessness, in their human desire to achieve a greater portion of freedom, will rise up in time and create their own. And because they've created it, and because it reflects their conception of justice, they will hold it more dearly.

We are best, in the world as it is now, as the beacon, not necessarily the bringer, of freedom. We are its friend, its exemplar, its encourager.

As a foreign policy this sounds, or has been made to sound, unduly passive. "You want us to sit around being a good example and the rest of them can take a hike." But if you want to be a beacon, it's actually a very hard job.

It involves its own activism. You can't be a beacon unless as a nation you're in pretty good shape. You can't be a beacon unless you send forth real light. You can't set an admirable example unless you're admirable. You can't be a beacon unless you really do inspire.

Do we always? No. We're not always a good example for the world. We have plenty of room for improvement. I'm being too jolly. We're a mess. We have a lot to clean up in our own house.

It would be good to have the most visible symbols of our country, the president and the Congress, be clean. So often they seem not to be. They are scandal-ridden, or an embarrassment, or seem in the eyes of the world to be bought and paid for by special interests or unions or industries or professions. Whether you are liberal or conservative, you agree it is important that the world be impressed by America's leaders, by their high-mindedness and integrity. Leaders who are not dragged through the mud because they actually don't bring much mud with them. There is room for improvement here.

To be a beacon is to speak softly to the world, with dignity, with elegance if you can manage it, or simple good-natured courtesy if you can't. A superpower should never shout, never bray, "We're number one!" If you're number one, you don't have to.

To be a beacon is to have a democracy in

which issues of actual import are regularly debated. Instead, much of our political coverage consists of daily disquisitions on "targeted ads," "narratives," and "positioning." We really do make politicians crazy. If a politician cares only about his ads and his rehearsed answers, the pundits call him inauthentic. But if a politician ignores these things to speak instead of great issues, we say he lacks "fire in the belly" and is incompetent. So many criticisms of politicians boil down to "He's not manipulating us well enough!"

We need more actual adults who are actually serious about the business of the nation.

To be a beacon is to keep the economic dream alive. We're still pretty good at this. The downside is the rise in piggishness that tends to accompany prosperity. It is not good to embarrass your nation with your greed. It disheartens those who are doing their best but are limited, or unlucky, or just haven't made it work yet. It is good when you have it not to keep it all but to help the limited, and unlucky, and those who just haven't made it work yet. Keep it going, Porky.

To be a beacon is to continue another thing we're good at, making the kind of citizens who go into the world and help it: the doctors, the scientists, the nurses. They choose to go and help. The world notices this, and says, "These are some kind of people, these Americans."

That is the greatest beacon-raising going on in America today. And yes, our soldiers do this too, in their kindness, in their hospital building, in their generosity.

To be a beacon is to support the creation of a culture that is not dark, or sulfurous, or obviously unwell. We introduce our culture to our new immigrants each day through television. Just for a moment, imagine you are a young person from Africa or South America, a new American. You come here and put on the TV—for even the most innocent know that TV is America and America is TV, and you want to learn quickly. What you see is an obvious and embarrassing obsession with sex, with sexual dysfunction, and with violence. You see the routine debasement of women parading as the liberation of women.

Conservatives have wrung their hands over this for a generation. For two, actually. But really, if you are a new immigrant to our country, full of hope, animated in part by some sense of mystery about this country that has lived in your imagination for twenty years, you have got to think: This is it? This ad for erectile dysfunction? Oh, I have joined something that is not healthy!

Sad to think this. They want to have joined a healthy and vibrant and well-balanced nation, not a sick circus.

I haven't even touched upon poverty, the material kind and the spiritual kind. I haven't touched on a lot.

But if we were to try harder to be better, if we were to try harder to be and seem as great as we are, we wouldn't have to bray so much about the superiority of our system. It would be obvious to all, as obvious as a big light in the darkness.

We not only should speak softly. We must also remember to speak. Not lecture or hector, but speak.

I remember two years ago when Hugo Chavez, the democratically elected president of Venezuela, population twenty-six million, which sells us at significant profit a lot of oil, spoke to the opening of the General Assembly of the United Nations.

The whole world was watching. Everyone knew he'd put on a show. This is what he said:

The "pretensions" of "the American empire" threaten "the survival" of mankind. The world must "halt this threat." The American president talks "as if he owned the world" and leads a "world dictatorship" that must not be allowed to "be consolidated." The U.S. government is "imperialist, fascist, assassin, genocidal," a "hypocritical" empire that only pretends to mourn the deaths of innocents. But not only the Mideast will rise. "People of the South," "oppressed" by America, must "strengthen ourselves, our will to do battle."

It wasn't at all vague. It was a call to arms.

The administration quickly moved to dismiss it: more bilge from the buffoon, more opera bouffe. We won't comment or dignify.

The American right didn't want to take him seriously (we don't need more problems), and the left doesn't want to see him clearly (we gave birth to that?). But Chavez's speech achieved some important objectives.

He raised his own standing. He got the world to look at him. He attempted to emerge as the heir to the dying Fidel Castro. Not the current Fidel, the old man in soft fatigues, but the Fidel of 1960, who when he went to the UN pointedly camped in a hotel in Harlem, and electrified the masses. Chavez even followed his speech with the announcement that he was giving heating oil to the needy of the Bronx. You know what they said in the Bronx? Thanks! It went over big on local TV.

Chavez's speech was, essentially if implicitly, a call to resistance, by any means, to the government of the United States. He made the argument that it is not America versus Saddam or America versus terrorists but the American Empire versus all the yearning people of the world. He claimed as his constituency everyone unhappy with the unipolar world.

He cleverly put some rhetorical distance between the current administration and the American people. This is not so much new as shrewd, and telling. It is an unacknowledged fact known to every diplomat in the world that the people of the world like Americans. Old Europe and New,

Africa, Asia, people on the ground all over, have some acquaintance with the particular American character of openness and generosity. We turn our faith, our yearning to make things better, and, no doubt, unease at our good fortune, into personal and private do-gooding. We send money, bring bandages, and overtip. We go to Africa and set up medical tents. We go to orphanages in far-off places and bring home children. The world has met us—and this, by the way, is our biggest foreign policy strength.

And so those who attack America, like Chavez, are forced to speak highly of Americans, which allowed him to reach some potential new allies here. People don't mind being told they are very fine but their government is very wicked. He also, in his mad intemperance, gave new cover to critics of America. Bashar Assad to Condoleezza Rice the next time he throws a snare: "You think I'm bad? Chavez would kill you!"

America has seen this before, seen Khrushchev bang his shoe on the table and say, "We will bury you." So it's tempting to think this is part of a meaningless stream of mischief.

But the temperature of the world is very

high, and maybe—again—we're not stuck in a meaningless stream but barreling down a dark corridor. The problem with heated words now is that it's not the old world anymore. In the old world, incompetent governments dragged cannons through the mud to set up a ragged front. Now every nut and nation wants, has, or is trying to get his hands on other weapons.

Harsh words inspire the unstable.

Coolants are needed.

My small idea is that we do not ignore the Chavezes of the future, but answer them. With the humility that comes with deep confidence, with facts, with truth. And with the implicit high regard that comes from, well, high regard.

If I am right, then civil defense must become not only a much higher priority in our country but a clearer one. The entire subject is bound down in some kind of governmental language of gobbledygook. But we should be creating—quietly—every day a great civil defense system, something that can help us when the bad days come.

It is fashionable to say, "Nothing can be done

to help if a suitcase bomb is used in a city." Really? No provisions, no food, no temporary shelters possible? No civil defense areas where it is ensured that the rule of law will prevail? There's nothing we can do?

What we need most in terms of civil defense are two words: presidential leadership. Nothing else will move this forward. Everything in this area is disjointed, chaotic, not thought through. As I've said, much time and money has been given to creating and funding studies and papers warning of this threat and that, suggesting this and that in response, and marked so deeply that it might as well be emblazoned on the cover of every report in forty-point type: "We in Congress have commissioned this study as a major ass-covering exercise so that if something happens and hundreds of thousands die, we can say: I told you this might happen!"

This is—how to put it?—not enough.

The general structure of our civil defense system consists of two parts, prevention of terror events and response to terror events. The first is aimed at stopping and disrupting attacks, the second at mitigating their consequences. The government gives more attention to deterrence than to response, which is exactly as it should be. Better to deter than to have to respond any day. But they are not giving enough attention to response, to preparedness.

It is not only the secondary concern of the government, it is too secondary. And I suspect part of the reason is psychological. To focus on response feels defeatist. It's like saying, "Um, we may not succeed in every attempt at deterrence." But we have to be adult, and serious. In the coming age we won't succeed in every attempt at deterrence.

This is where presidential leadership—presidential persistence, even preoccupation—is needed.

Current civil defense planning gives little thought to mass public stores of goods, of food, water, and alternate energy, of sites of congregation. It is not clear that any preparation for truly mass catastrophes is effectively organized.

After 9/11, gas masks were distributed to Congress and the Pentagon. Steps were taken to ensure continuity of government. HHS rushed to fill stockpiles of vaccines for potential biological attacks involving smallpox and anthrax. (The last didn't work out; in 2006 an order of seventy-five million doses of anthrax vaccine had to be cancelled because of contracting problems.)

You remember that some individuals after 9/11 decided on their own to acquire various means of protection, such as gas masks, but the government didn't see and has not seen such expenditures as necessary or desirable. Which is funny, because they thought it necessary and desirable for members of Congress. The returns on outfitting millions of citizens for attacks have not been judged by the government to be efficient. But—forgive me—since when has the Bush administration and its Congresses been interested in efficiency and cost?

What some experts worry about most, in terms of terrorist threats, is a biological attack. The reasons: accessibility, and a lower threshold of operational success.

The federal government claims it has stockpiled enough smallpox vaccine to vaccinate every U.S. resident. That's good, because most U.S. residents need it. If you were vaccinated forty years ago, it's worn off; and we stopped vaccinating kids in 1972, because the disease had been eradicated. So . . . in a way, no one's vaccinated anymore, and if the toxin were released, it would be very bad. The government knows this. In 2002 and 2003 the government started a new program whereby first-responders and military personnel would receive smallpox shots. This would increase preparedness in case of a biological attack. That was good too. But smallpox shots are not available to the general public. Why? The government believes there are too many risks associated with general vaccinations, such as having someone develop smallpox in reaction to the shot and spreading it to others. But when the five hundred thousand first-responders, medical professionals, and members of the military were vaccinated, it didn't lead to outbreaks of smallpox. Really—I think we would have read about it in the papers! The government insists that if there were a smallpox attack, they would at that time make the vaccine available to everyone.

I live in New York. Imagine a bioterrorism attack—smallpox, say, in Queens. It's nice to imagine that people would peacefully line up somewhere (by the way, where? In what places?)

and that thousands of personnel with all the supplies they needed (who are they? where did they all of a sudden come from?) would treat citizens quickly and with dispatch, and that a trusting, peaceful populace would wait their turn (Queens? New York?) and that no problems would ensue. But somehow I don't imagine it that way. Do you? I'm not even sure the federal government has quite enough vaccine for three hundred million people. I only hope that it is true.

There are more questions than answers here. Only presidents can get the questions answered.

Here is the testimony of former deputy assistant to the president, and Homeland Security advisor on the White House staff, Richard A. Falkenrath, speaking in March 2006, to a U.S. Senate committee on the inadequacies of preparedness: "The National Response Plan is not adequate for catastrophic disease contingencies . . . particularly those which will require the effective distribution of life-saving medicines to a fearful population over very large areas in very short periods of time. . . . The Department of Defense should be directed to plan and prepare for the assumption of . . . responsibilities—to include the provision of essential health care, distribution of medical countermeasures, rationing of scarce essential supplies—and to anticipate the inability of state, local and private-sector entities to perform the medical and logistical functions expected of them in the National Response Plan."

That sounds right. But someone powerful has to care enough to make it happen.

What civil defense planning actually usually consists of right now in America is people having a sleepless night surfing websites looking for what they'll need to survive if a hard time ever comes.

We can do better.

A final note on the Department of Homeland Security, which is charged with many preparedness responsibilities. If it will not set back the movement for civil defense, maybe it's time to admit that the Department of Homeland Security is one of the huge messes of the Bush years, that it didn't work, doesn't work, that it wastes money, that it's been blasted for wasting the funds it's given each year on useless pork. It's a big gargantuan mess with so many moving parts that it seems incapable of doing very much at all successfully. Also it is my view that it is the Indian burial ground of the hackocracy.

My DHS anecdote. Once, two high DHS officials invited me to talk to them about my concerns. This was five years ago. I had plenty. If you went to the DHS website, for instance, you couldn't find advice on what to do if a suitcase nuke went off in your city; all you could find on the front page was press releases on how wonderful DHS was. You have to do better, I said. They took notes, which was gratifying. Then they got to the heart of the meeting. One of them wanted to write a book about being a "security mom" who spends her time trying to save the nation while balancing the needs of home and family. Did I think that was a good idea? I wish I could say that I said, "Well, as a taxpayer and lover of my country I have to go kill myself now." But I didn't. I just wished her well and left somewhat depressed. I should not have been. People are people: they always forget the mission. They have to be reminded.

Memo to the next president: Break up DHS into coherent individual departments that have clear-line responsibilities, and will be subject to clear-line accountability. Take it apart, make it work, and—this is very important—get rid of the Nazi-ish name. "Homeland" is barely an American word, and not an American concept. And even if it were, Homeland Security has come to sound like one word to everyone in the country, and that word is: failure.

Allow me to indulge what is and has been for me, for years, a preoccupation. It is with our electrical grid. Its well-being is a central civil defense issue.

Everything in America runs on electricity. Communications—the phone, the TV, the radio, the Internet. The lights, the heat, the ATM, the bank, the pump, the refrigerator. The machines in the operating room, the lights on the runway. As I type I listen to music that is plugged in, on a machine that is plugged in, under lights that are plugged in. I receive word from people I care about through two machines that are, at the moment, plugged in and being recharged.

If something bad happens we will get information, instructions, inspiration, and help from things that are plugged in. And we will be largely without information, instruction, data, assistance, and inspiration if the grid goes down.

Everything. Depends. On. Electricity.

Even poets have noticed. Well, one poet, Lawrence Ferlinghetti, a great figure of the 1950s counterculture who was interviewed in 2005 by *The New York Times* on the occasion of his receiving a lifetime achievement award from the National Book Foundation. He agreed it was "gratifying" to receive it, added that the word sounded "fatuous," and noted, "[I]t's high time we honored this endangered species." What species, poets? "No, the literarians in the world, and there are millions of them. They are not considered the dominant culture in this country. What's called the dominant culture will fade away as soon as the electricity goes off." There was more, and it was pretty wonderful, but the point is . . . this is a man who knows what electricity has done and become in our country, and this is a man who perhaps was suggesting he knows it will go off.

I kept this interview taped to a wall in my kitchen for years.

(Let me add parenthetically that Ferlinghetti

went on to say the message of the 1960s was: Be Here Now. The message of the current era, with "the cellphones, the fax, the Internet, the whole schmear—the slogan you have today is 'Be Somewhere Else Now.'" How beautifully observed is that?)

Two years ago I went to a small congressional group, about a dozen aides and staffers, to talk a little about my fears for our country. I said, to their surprise, that a primary concern of mine was electricity, and how much we depend on it, and how frail and vulnerable the system on which we depend is. "You doing something to strengthen the grid?" I asked. Blank faces. Silence. Then a bright young woman said she thought there'd been something about electricity in the big appropriations bill a while back.

I remember it so well in part because I realized only after my question was answered how desperate I was to hear, "Hell, yes, it's a major concern up here. We've just okayed funding to rebuild the grid top to bottom." I am exactly like any other American: I always want to think my government is on the case.

There is near-universal agreement among experts that the national grid is in bad shape—aging, overstretched, overburdened, inefficient. And vulnerable not only in case of terrorist attacks but also to cyber attacks. (There's been some attention paid to the grid since the 2003 blackout, and improvements have been made, but not enough.)

And you know the American leader who has engaged passionately on this issue, with focus and leadership, breaking through as Mr. Electricity and forcing people to focus on the grid? Yes, I believe that would be: no one.

You know how often Mr. McCain and Mr. Obama have spoken of the national grid? Yes, I believe that would be: zero.

Let's play nightmare. Something happens in New York. You've been watching cable TV, on CNN, from the Time Warner building. There's a sort of blip on the screen, and then it goes dark. You go to MSNBC, from out of Rockefeller Center. Blank. You go to a major network. Blank. You surf, looking for a news show based in Washington. The anchor is looking distracted and saying, "We've got reports of something going on in New

York and we're—" And then that goes blank. Then a sputter, and lights out everywhere. Everything off. The radio? You forgot the batteries. The neighbors? They're stuck in the elevator. Darkness descends, no word in or out, streets dark . . . and this goes on for days. Then weeks. Maybe at some point you'll get news of what happened: a suitcase bomb, a mass cyber attack, a terror event of some sort. And maybe by the time you get word, things will have turned very difficult indeed.

The grid is so vulnerable that the Council on Foreign Relations noted in April 2007, "Current stresses on the U.S. energy grid present cause for concern. . . . The specter of terrorism also looms large: Experts say jihadis in Iraq have proven adept at disrupting the electrical grid in that country. . . . the system that carries electricity from producers to consumers . . . is in dire straits."

It is one thing to sigh over the fact that we are vulnerable to blackouts in the height of summer, with everyone's air conditioner blasting. It's another thing to say we're vulnerable to having our electricity taken away during a terror event, or as part of one.

It's one thing to say the marvelous and stoic American people will take it like the champs they are, and that no civil or societal disturbances will follow a broad or national loss of electrical power for weeks, or even months.

But it's another thing to live it.

We need presidential-level leadership here. Desperately.

Trust me. Something like this is going to happen, in our lifetimes.

Whatever the cost—*whatever the cost*—it will be worth it to take actions that can strengthen and restrengthen the American electrical system.

These are a few, very few, ideas, areas that I think could be explored to our benefit. Maybe, as you read, you are coming up with a better list. Good, lists are a beginning.

I'd quickly add another, myself. America has to relearn how to make things again. Once, we were a great industrial nation; now we are a great information age nation. There used to be more Americans who could build a small house than stand up and speak in public. Now it's the other way around. We are great talkers. More of us have to learn how to make things again. We have all had a moment where we thought, "If I were president I'd . . ." Well, if I were president I would decree that Shop and Home Ec be returned to the core curriculum of all American public schools, as they were thirty years ago. Only, this time, boys and girls could choose either or both. My twenty-one-year-old son's friends will probably be businessmen, lawyers, teachers. Good, they'll all be needed in the future. But so will carpenters, builders, welders of steel, people who can pour a foundation, people who can make things. Including a meal. Is it not in our national interest to encourage such education?

So: we have much to do. And it all starts with a greater civility, a greater respect, both a higher—and deeper—tone to our political conversation.

I should end by noting the obvious. We'll get through the bad time. We'll get through it, whatever happens. We are America. There's a lot of ruin in a nation, as Adam Smith said. Great countries can take a lot of punishment, recover from a lot of loss. There's a vast amount of ruin in us. We are a great nation populated by a gifted and still-gritty people. We have deep spiritual resources, great natural resources, a sturdy system of laws, enduring traditions of generosity and support, and military and technological prowess and might.

But we can make things better now. We can be moving to make our country stronger now. We can focus now, so that we can more readily endure into the next good time.

For that too is coming.

We just have to get there.

A few days after 9/11 I bought at a little shop something someone had made at home, a big safety pin from which hung eight smaller safety pins the same size, each covered in little red, white, and blue beads. I wore it almost every day for a long time, years. A safety pin holds things together. It was a way of saying: Our country will hold together. People stopped me everywhere to find where they could get one. At some point, and in the way of things, I stopped remembering to wear it, and at some point I put it away in an old jewelry box.

But in the writing of this book I went and took it out and showed it to a friend, and now . . . well, now I am wearing it again. We are a great nation and a great people and we have got to hold together. That's all it means. But then, as meanings go, you don't get much bigger than that.